*An aggie, who's
gone straight
Best wishes*

Jackalope
Ca$ino

Richard E Peck

Richard E. Peck

REPertory Publishing

Placitas New Mexico

© 2010 by Richard E. Peck
All rights reserved
First edition
Library of Congress Cataloguing-in-Publication Data
Peck, Richard E.
Jackalope Ca$ino / Richard E. Peck—first edition

ISBN 978-0-9726308-1-8 (trade paperback)
ISBN 978-0-9726308-2-5 (cloth)

1 3 5 7 9   10 8 6 4 2

Printed and Bound in the USA by Lightning Source
Set in Minion Pro
Design and Composition: Earl Mason and Barbara Haines
Printed in the United States

Jackalope Ca$ino is a work of fiction. The characters, events, and locations portrayed herein are fictional or are used fictionally. Any noticeable misrepresentations are—in Kurt Vonnegut's term—"foma."

This one's for

Pat Longoria

and

Brad Snyder

who have enriched our family.

Books by Richard E. Peck

Philly Amateurs
—"filled with fun...great characterization" Lola R. Eagle
—"another larcenous gem [by] New Mexico's answer to Donald Westlake"
Robert Kresge, retired CIA analyst

Strategy of Terror
—"Peck gets better with every book." *Reading New Mexico*
—"pace is superb...dialogue sparkles" Amazon review

Dead Pawn
—"crisp, succinct description, realistic dialogue,...wit and candor...
authentic feel" Carrie Seidman, *Alb. Tribune*
—"dead-on believable" Robert Mayer, *Santa Fe New Mexican*

Something for Joey
—"touching story about courage and the love between siblings" K. Smith,
Amazon review
—"most compelling story I have read" Steven Winegar

Final Solution
—"Peck plunges into the genre of science fiction and, as with all his books,
comes up a winner." *Reading New Mexico*
—"a swift, bright narrative style...coruscating sense of humor...fistful of
genius for characterization...a fine feel for language" Theodore Sturgeon,
Galaxy Magazine

All the Courses in the Kingdom
— " ... one of the true hidden gems for any globe-trotting golfer['s] library"
Bob Fagan Reviews
—"even the non-golfer will enjoy...this book" Lola Eagle

The New Mexico Experience
—"perhaps the best book...on the cultural history of New Mexico" William
Maryott, Amazon review

Traveling at My Desk
—"What a delight! Who needs Lake Wobegon when your desk is around?"
Stanley Krippner, PhD. author of *Dreamworking*
—"Peck's adroit writing will make you laugh out loud." Drusilla Claridge,
author of *Peacock Ore*

§ 1 §

Two curves east of Tramway, driving upslope over the access road to the tram base-station, Wince checked his mirror and flinched to see the white Crown Vic behind them. Again.

Same car. Black sidewall tires, no wheel covers, dented left front fender…a cop. It was Chutters just pulling into the deep shadow of Sandia Ridge stretching west toward the Rio Grande.

Wince glanced at Leela Begay beside him.

She hadn't noticed.

He said nothing. No point over-reacting. He focused on the twisting access road ahead and pushed the Mustang harder upslope toward the Sandia ridge. Here outside the Albuquerque city limits, Chutters wouldn't ticket him, or shouldn't. Wince went lead-foot and topped 50 in a 30 mph zone. He focused on the shadowed slope ahead.

This time of day, "Sandia" didn't describe the mountain ridge well. But in the evening, with the setting sun west of anyone facing these abrupt and stony cliffs, the entire ridge wore the pink glow that made the 15th century Spanish explorers name these the "watermelon" mountains.

Bob Wince drove his Mustang higher up slope into the shadow, now topping 70 mph. Almost squatting on the curves, the Mustang held so tight to the road that Wince felt

1

the imperfections in the macadam surface sending tremors through the steering wheel. One glance in the mirror told him that Chutters had dropped back but kept coming.

Leela caught him checking the mirror. "Is there a problem?" she said, and tugged her seat belt tighter.

"No, no. Nothing." He shook his shoulders to loosen up and sat tall. No reason to spook her.

He'd talked her into lunch at High Finance, the restaurant perched a mile above them at the end of the tram ride. Probably a mistake. It was a workday, or should be, mid-week with his Albuquerque crew neck-deep into both construction projects he had underway: a motel remodel; and work on the restaurant he wanted to unload. It was the wrong time to take a day off from work. Even a half-day. But…he'd promised her.

"You want to go back?" Leela said.

How'd she do that? Like reading his mind. "No," he said. "It'll be okay."

Her smile said she'd seen through his unconcern but she'd let it pass.

Parked in the dusty lot at the base of the tram, he spotted Chutters' traffic-weary Crown Vic idling on a cushion of black exhaust smoke back at the lot entrance. Sitting there. A presence.

They climbed the wooden stairs to join the short queue of tourists entering the tramcar and peered up the steep slope. From the base they could see only as far as the first cable tower standing tall above the rock-crusted mountainside. "Here in the front," Wince said, urging her toward the forward window. "Watch the slope sliding under us while we climb. We'll see the city view on the way back down."

Leela leaned against him and rested both hands on the grip bar at the bottom edge of the plexiglass window. She looked up at the steel cable above them, pointing their way up the mountain.

When the cable drew taut on its huge drum and the tramcar trembled on the verge of flight, the boy who'd loaded them aboard said, "All set?" He latched and locked the sliding door.

The car lurched away from the loading dock into its climb to the docking station high atop the Sandia ridge. Passengers grunted at the jolt. Two white-haired matrons seized the handrail along the starboard side windows to steady themselves. A young man in khaki cargo shorts and a muscle shirt snickered. Nothing was going to faze him.

"Our flight will take...oh...fifteen minutes," their guide said. "It's non-stop...usually." A good-looking kid with skateboarder's blond bangs over one eye, he seemed to strut, standing at the door. He was entertaining them with his canned speech. "We'll be traveling two and a half miles, over the world's longest aerial tram line. We climb from six thousand feet to ten-five at the top...if nothing goes wrong...this time."

Wince had heard the rehearsed wit before. He craned to look past the station roofline and saw Chutters' unmarked Ford leave the lot and head back downslope. Wince knew they'd see him again.

After a year of Chutters' shadow at his back, Wince no longer puzzled over the periodic appearances. A year earlier, fresh out of state prison thanks to early release, Wince had walked into this father's restaurant to find Chutters an uninvited part of the welcoming party, Chutters and his partner, Somethingorother Cordova, two of Albuquerque's finest.

"Hey, Dimmie. Is this your boy?"

Before his father could say anything, Wince waved in a curt greeting and said, "Bob Wince." He didn't offer his hand.

"We heard you were in Santa Fe," Cordova said. "How'd that go?"

Wince shrugged.

"He asked a question," Chutters said. "That calls for an answer." When none came forth, he stared at Wince, then said, "I'm Dan Chutters."

Dimmie interrupted. "It's good to see you, Dan." He turned to call out, "Janie! Two large coffees, to go."

Chutters stepped closer. "Keep the coffee. We're here because two of your customers had their home burglarized while they were eating here. Kinda makes me wonder how the thieves knew exactly when the victims would be away from home. Maybe somebody phoned 'em?"

"Dad?" Wince hooked a thumb toward the kitchen. "I'll be in the back."

"Hiding?" Cordova smiled. "It won't help."

"This time it's Dimmie we want to talk to," Chutters said, "But your turn will come."

Wince knew that was true.

Leela caught him musing. "Why's that cop still on your case? Isn't he one who arrested those two crooks you told him about?"

"Dan Chutters. Patrolman then, detective now. He and his partner made the arrest."

"Thanks to you."

"No good deed goes unpunished."

"So why's he harassing you."

"Maybe not harassing. Just 'keeping track.' He's probably even a good guy, but he's all cop. And he's gone now." He pointed at the departing Crown Vic.

"What's he think you've done?"

"Not to worry."

"Uh-huh," she said, unpersuaded.

Their guide coughed for attention. "My name's Mike Baca, and I'll be your crew for flight number"—he checked his clipboard—"flight number seven." He rattled off the familiar spiel Wince expected. Fifteen degrees colder up top, a good chance of spotting wildlife in the canyons below, a dozen varieties of cactus from chain *cholla* to *agave* and cow's tongue scattered among the boulders.

Only sixteen passengers, half the number that rode most afternoon flights. The usual gaggle of tourists. Retired couples, or vacationers, a pregnant girl holding hands with the guy in cargo shorts. Usual types, no obvious celebrities.

Wince watched Baca scan the sparse crowd until the kid's gaze settled on Leela Begay. Wince didn't blame him. Striking in her beauty, the only Navajo in this morning's gathering of Anglo tourists, Leela earned stares even in groups much bigger than this. Wince leaned close to whisper to her. "Looks like you've got a fan."

"Got a question, Miss?" Baca smiled.

She shook her head, then caught Wince checking his

watch. "Bob? Where would you rather be?" she said.

"Say what?"

"You've been reading your watch, like we're late. You look up at the ridge, the watch...." She turned away, aloof, the way she got when she was upset. He hoped she might only be showing Indian-cool.

Wince hoped, but he knew better. He was screwing up. He frowned at Baca. No one else here he could blame for his mistakes.

Baca shrugged. "Enjoy the view from the crest, eleven thousand square miles, more than a hundred miles in any direction," he said. "Have lunch at *High Finance* up top, and I'll be back up on flight number ten—little over an hour—if you want to ride down with me then."

The radio under his bench seat interrupted with static. "Mike, come in. Report."

"No wind at tower one," Baca said into the microphone. "It's dead calm." He tucked away the clipboard and thumbed the radio silent. "Miss? Come check it out." He beckoned Leela and pointed to the slope below them where a scrawny tan coyote scrambled and juked around the jumbled rocks.

"We see it," Wince said. He took Leela's arm.

"Sorry." Baca went after the old ladies standing beside him. They were goggle-eyed and edgy. "See that dead piñon below tower number two?" he said. "Sometimes there's an eagle roosts there. Soaking up the sunshine."

The tramcar approached tower two. They saw flight number six empty,swinging side to side in its descent toward them. Baca offered a warning: "You'll feel a little jolt here."

Passengers braced and uttered a gasp, as the tram car

lurched past the tower and dipped into its bellied final ascent. An instant of stomach-wrenching free fall, followed by the steady tug up a long sweeping stretch of shimmering cable.

"That's your thrill for the day," Baca said.

"From here to the top it's a steady ride on a one-point-seven mile stretch of cable. Over a thousand feet above the ground most of the way." He pointed out the cactus-dotted jumble of rocks below, then toward the tramcar swinging its way off the crest.

"Here's flight number six, coming down. It's empty now, but..." Baca abandoned his spiel when the buzz of blurted conversation drowned him out.

This was the spot, halfway up, where Wince had heard passengers on other flights step up the volume, chattering reassurance to cover their uncertain fears. It was the altitude that got to them, swinging free over the rocks so far below. The older man near the door started to whistle.

"Does that skinny cable there ever break?" Cargo Shorts asked, flexing his fearlessness.

"Not today," Baca said. "But the day's still young."

Leela smiled. Wince leaned a shoulder into her and turned her to face uphill, like a quarter horse cutting a single calf from the herd.

"Can we see the ledge?" She asked. "You know...where the hang gliders jump off?"

Wince shrugged his backpack higher and pointed. "North," he said. "Just short of the radio and TV relay towers. That's the highest part of the mountain. They go off toward the west, into the thermals...the updraft. Hang gliders, and base jumpers, they all—."

"*They* do? Don't you and Leon Quintana do that?"

"We *did* that. A couple of times, when park rangers weren't around. They don't hassle hang gliders, but there's no more base jumping from the ridge."

"You jumped anyway," Leela said, "Macho-foolish."

"For kicks," he said, quickly covering his embarrassment with boasting. "Leon talked me into it. Kind of like a dare. You know, when you're twenty-five and think you're immortal, you do dumb things."

She poked him in the ribs. "And it's just as foolish to go hiking that narrow trail up on top."

"It's not that narrow."

She looked her doubt at him.

"And all that's past. You know what the fine is, they catch you base jumping here?"

"Forget the fine. Why risk your neck?"

"I'll show you the jump-off when we get to the restaurant." He shrugged to resettle his pack again. His chute case, it hung loose without the chute and slider in it. Light, it felt awkward. Not much in it. A bottle of Dasani, her sweater, his wind shirt. He checked his watch, near noon already. Elliott Chávez would be at the motel job-site. If he and Leela hurried lunch he knew he could get back and help Elliott and the crew.

"Bob?" She nudged him. "You with me?"

"Yeah, good." Wince leaned against the window and reached down to take her hand. He laid it on the plexiglass. "Feel the vibration? We'll shake, landing in the dock. You'll be okay."

"I love landing. It's flying that scares me."

The tramcar jerked and shuddered and thumped into the dock. Passengers pressed toward the door until Baca raised his hand. "In a minute," he said. He unlocked the door and slid it open. A gust of cool air filled the cabin with the dusty scent of piñon. "Watch your step here. The restrooms are straight ahead. Restaurant to your left. And from the walkway you can see the ski slopes down the east side."

Wince watched Baca hand Cargo Shorts and the pregnant girl over to his partner on the plank loading dock, holding her arm. The old ladies went next. The short one slipped Baca a dollar. He smiled his thanks.

"I'll be heading down soon. Then back up in an hour," Baca said. He turned his smile on Leela and said, "Wait for me? We'll ride down together."

Wince pointed at Baca and said, "I don't think so." No smile, cold eyes, no debate on this. Time for Baca to get the message. Wince handed Leela her red sweater and helped her out onto the plank deck.

Baca shrugged as the two passed by. He turned an innocent gaze on the cloudless sky.

As much as Wince would rather be at work, the view from the plank walkway was worth the trip, even in the cool breeze that stirred Leela's black tresses and made her snug the sweater closer around her shoulders. Beyond Albuquerque lying thousands of feet below them, beyond the Rio Grande that separates the city from its western suburbs, beyond the black-rimmed craters of the extinct volcanoes on the near horizon, ninety miles west stood the snow-dusted dome of Mount Taylor. Even father away were the *Sangre de Cristos* and the high mesa that masked Los Alamos. North lay Santa

Fe and the ski slopes, bare of snow now. The Navajo reservation due west—the *Diné* homeland bordered by four sacred mountains—was too distant to be seen.

But Wince felt Leela peer that way, even as she snuggled against him. It was a habit she might not admit to. Many *Diné* were uncomfortable away from Window Rock. Edgy. Even Leela. In the months they'd been going together—*almost* together—she'd ignored his suggestions that she move to Albuquerque. Maybe not move in with him, but at least live nearer. The three-hour drive to Window Rock was getting old.

"I'm just sorry we're here to late to catch the short shadow," Wince said. The breeze had picked up, making his eyes water. "You cold?"

Leela shivered and brushed tousled hair out of her eyes. "What shadow?" She pointed to the wash of sunlight on the plank platform at their feet.

"The shadow sweep," Wince said. "Early, almost every morning. My dad loved it. The sun rises back here, east of the Sandias, and the ridge casts this amazing long shadow across the river all the way to the west mesa, black at first, turning purple. You sit watching the west edge of the shadow backing east toward you as the sun gets higher over the mountain, and the long shadow gets shorter. It's slow at first, then faster, till...*whoosh!* There's a rush maybe a hundred miles an hour and the shadow swoops back over you and disappears. The whole valley lights up in a flash. You feel the sun on the back of your neck."

"That's your 'shadow sweep'?"

"I see it every morning. Up here on the ridge the shadow

gets shorter and shorter, pinching till it disappears." And now...he spread his hands wide. "Full sun."

"Are you trying to work me?" She turned him with a hand on his waist, using him as a windscreen, "You think this shadow stuff is romantic. Or maybe you're going mystic on me."

"Me?" No way he'd admit she was right. He shook his head. "Buck Tsosie said you'd like to see the 'time of no shadows.' The perfect center of the day, he called it, with morning behind you and afternoon ahead." And then he was sorry he'd mentioned Buck. There was something between the two of them, Buck and Leela. Something besides their common heritage.

"Come on!" She laughed it off.

"No, really. Buck's got this thing about the Sandia ridge. Maybe it's not 'magic,' but it's a 'place of good consequences,' he calls it. The atmosphere, here in the sky."

"Buck was playing the 'wise old In'jun.' He sent us up here, out of his hair, so he can work on the restaurant without you 'supervising.'"

Wince draped an arm over her shoulders. "You want to go check on him?"

"He and Elliott are your partners. Trust them or don't. It's not up to me."

Wince heard the edge in her comment. He thought he detected jealousy, too, a funny reaction. Another woman might get it. He didn't.

She didn't drop it. "How many partners have you got? You and Rolan still have Albuquerque's finest on your back about the turquoise-that cop Chutters. You and Elliott are remodeling the motel shell. You and Buck are re-doing your dad's restaurant." She displayed a fan of open fingers. "Count 'em," she said. "It's a wonder you've got any time for me. Aren't we kind of like 'partners?'"

Not going well. Wince searched for the answer that wouldn't provoke her. "Lunch partners," he said. "And that's more important than the others. *You're* more important." He turned to face her, but she pulled away.

"Okay, you promised me lunch to get me up here. Now pay up...*partner*."

He took a cell phone out of his shirt pocket. "Let me tell Elliott I'll be late."

Her laugh was rueful, but it was a laugh. "Lunch first," she said. She snatched the phone from him and tugged him toward the restaurant.

$ 2 $

Since the day he got fired for what he still considered a simple indiscretion, T.J. David had been waiting for a phone call. *The* phone call. Bounced out of his corporate suite at *The Shangri-La*, unemployed, bedded down in a crummy $40 a night fleabag south of the Vegas strip, he'd waited. Why the delay? Mr. Tesdescu had accepted his explanation, and apology…or had seemed to. But how long was David supposed to appreciate that? The hunky clotheshorse was collecting his pound of flesh by making David wait for a summons. Sweating him.

The time hadn't all been wasted. David used it to make plans. First, find a way to recover the old man's million, some way Mr. Tedescu couldn't take over. And the old hunky would try. David knew that.

Failure wasn't an acceptable option. Mr. Tedescu would back him only so long. And *The Shangri-La*'s California owners, the money men, considered David's 'indiscretion' a real fuck-up. They were unhappy, their unhappiness squelched by Mr. Tedescu. For now.

So except for one three-day trip into Arizona, David had waited in the motel room, with its rattling air conditioner. Watching the crap on day time television, practicing his one-hand cut: left hand, right, left, then double-cut with the right. Shuffling the cards, waiting. Dealing seconds, for the practice. Playing solitaire. He won every deal. He cheated.

The call woke him on a Thursday morning, five weeks after The Commission gigged him for his mistake. Not a real mistake. He'd mollified an angry loser to take some sting out of the moron's losing streak by giving him a win. Nothing all that special. He'd rigged a lottery and let the loser drive away a new Hummer. Anyway, somebody had to win the over-priced gas guzzler. The bastards in Newport Beach should have thanked David for his initiative. No harm done…until the lottery staffer who'd pulled off the rigged lottery drawing got shit-faced drunk. He bragged about palming the winning ticket he drew out of the glass drum, then blamed David for the idea.

It got them both fired from *The Shangri-La*. There was no arrest, two hours of questioning but no arrest. An agreement was reached with the Regulatory Commission. Mr. Tedescu's apes beat the shit out of the lottery staffer and dumped him in the desert but let David off. The casino fired him, jerked his Nevada license, paid the fine levied by the Commission.

Lifetime banishment and the fine: one million bucks.

Mr. Tedescu paid it, himself, told David to wait, then refused to see him again. Made him wait and sweat, for five weeks, till now. It meant Mr. Tedescu owned him. Now, finally, he was calling David in.

David took a cab—his Corvette was gone, a small but painful down payment on his debt—and then fumed for more than two hours in the waiting room outside Mr. Tedescu's private office on the second floor of *The Shangri-La*. The receptionist, a real piece of eye candy and new since David's firing, ignored him. She was part of the décor: diamond chip earrings, silicone chest, brilliant green contact lenses, scarlet lipstick under a shadowed upper lip. Very decorative but retard-vague, nodding over magazine photos while she mouthed the text.

A blinking light over the double doors to Mr. Tedescu's inner office broke her trance. "Mr. Tedescu will see you now, Mr…" she said. She didn't bother to look up when she said it, letting David know how little he mattered in the grand scheme of things. Her spotless desktop held only a telephone, her folded hands, and the tattered copy of *Tiger Beat* that kept her rapt attention. Her head bobbed in time to thumping disco drivel surging from unseen speakers. She waved him across the room, said, "Through that door," and deigned to look up. Her superior smile said 'I'll let you see him, whoever you are.'

"About fucking time," David said. He'd been through 'that door' hundreds of times before this piece of meat ever came to work here. He didn't move from the Bauhaus chair where he'd just wasted two miserable hours on the two-minute job of cataloguing the sparse décor of this sterile, windowless anteroom. "What's your name?" he said. He waited for her attention.

"Sheree." She frowned . "Why do—"

"Well, Sher*eeeeee*." *Now* he walked close to lean over her desk. "If you decide against electrolysis, you ought to buy some moustache wax." He rubbed his upper lip in demonstration and winked at her.

Now, she was looking at him.

"The name is 'David.' Remember it, when you drag your

ass out to find your next job. Tee Jay David," he said. He crossed to the heavy double doors and tugged them open.

Mr. Tedescu sat behind a single horizontal sheet of plate glass resting on eight gleaming copper legs. Beyond him, against a windowless wall in this square room—20 by 20 feet, David guessed—was a half-size replica of the glass-and-copper table/desk. It held two telephones and a tan calfskin attaché case, cocked open to reveal a few papers inside. Beside the smaller table was a document shredder. When the papers in the attaché case had been studied and their contents committed to Mr. Tedescu's incredible memory, they would be fed through the gleaming, chattering teeth of the shredder. And Mr. Tedescu would go home, to his third floor suite at *The Shangri-La*, finished for the day.

On the way he might drop down a floor to check out the lounge acts or walk through the casino gaming areas, a trip he took no more than twice a week. He disliked facing the crowds in his casino…but he disliked even more the occasional lack of a crowd in his casino. Either way, face time on the floor was time wasted. The players wouldn't recognize him. And it disgusted him to see them praying to the dice or trying to count the aces and faces in a six-deck shoe.

"You asked me to come in?"

Mr. Tedescu didn't look up from his desk. He pointed at the spot on the floor where he wanted David to stand. And wait.

David knew the man watched everything, from his office, on twelve wall-mounted flat TV screens. Mr. Tedescu had shown him the set-up, less information than threat.

"Every inch of the place," he'd said. "Wherever the action

is, wherever you are, wherever I want to check, I can see it all." He'd waved a hand over this eye in the sky.

The pictures cycled throughout the casino, switching past a dozen views that four alternating pairs of security men, elsewhere on this floor, monitored 24 hours a day. Mr. Tedescu watched action on the floor to get a feel for the take.

He was content to trust the day's-end soft income summaries from the six department managers. The "hard" numbers became the next day's workload him, placed in a thin neat stack within the attaché case, after recording the numbers in the two sets of books he kept.

Mr. Tedescu began to hum. No telling what. "In a minute," he said.

Even after all his visits to this office, David found each summons unique and unexpected, each interview bizarre. Mr. Tedescu was rail-thin and dressed to impress, though for days on end he met face-to-face with no one. He was always a vision in monochrome, always, garments dyed to match like that old golf pro, Doug Sanders.

David had seen him in lime green one day, peach or golf, or solid black from head to toe. He pictured the sorbet counter at Baskins-Robbins, a vision interrupted when he watched a second man enter the room through the double doors and stand against the right-hand wall.

"Artie Files," Mr. Tedescu said, after a moment. "He's your new driver. He stays with you."

"Driver?" David said. "I don't need—"

"And bodyguard. Insurance, in a way. He'll protect my investment in you, Tee Jay. Until we work out the details of my recompense."

"How you doing?" Files nodded to David and posed, standing at ease, hands clasped behind him. He wore Nike trainers and a banana-yellow tracksuit. Broad shoulders, narrow waist, a living traffic yield sign. He stood shifting from one foot to the other, the pound of gleaming gaudy bling at his neck swinging back and forth. A white guy, dressed rapper black.

There were no chairs in the office, except for the throne on which Mr. Tedescu perched, elevated on a foot-high platform. He could look down on anyone summoned before him

"Have you anything to tell me?" Mr. Tedescu asked.

David glanced at Files. "In private?"

Mr. Tedescu chewed his cheek and considered the request. He nodded and motioned Files from the room. "Outside, Artie."

§ 3 §

Wince sat with his back to the window to give Leela the view of the western horizon, over his shoulder. Leela sat across from him. He leaned back to enjoy her. The noon sun warmed Wince's back and lit her in a spotlight.

Lella Begay was twenty-five, glowing golden, with eyes black as her shining hair, reservation born and raised, an ASU graduate, teacher in the Window Rock tribal school, and tougher, smarter, more independent than such a sketchy biography promised. Wince didn't blame the Baca kid on the tramcar for hitting on her.

Wince had done the same thing the first time he saw her. With the same result. She'd answered his come-on in *Diné*, like she didn't speak English. Chilled him out. He replayed the memory.

Lunch over now, the clatter of wait staff clearing tables spread a soft mutter in the high-ceilinged room. He relaxed in the comforting aroma of baked apples. A dessert left unfinished on the nearest table.

"Hey, Buster." She rapped her glass with a spoon. "You've stopped listening again. What's on your mind?"

"I think you ought to move to Albuquerque. We need teachers here, too."

"And you're tired of the drive up to the rez."

"Six or more hours on the road, round-trip."

"Avoid it. Move out to Window Rock." She cocked her head and smiled, waiting.

He shrugged. "No, no chance. Not till I remodel or unload *Half-Off*. Until I get somebody to run it, get the motel apartments finished, until—"

"You mean until 'never.' Why do—"

"No, I mean until some day. Maybe."

"Seriously? You might move?"

"You'd help me turn Navajo?"

"We're not bigots. We let you palefaces live with us. Just not those guys from Vegas." She slid her flan across the table. "Want a bite?"

He shook his head and pushed it back. "They're still hanging around?"

"I knew you weren't listening. I told you, the whole crew of them came in last spring, after the council changed their tune."

"Changed, how?"

"They surrendered! They said okay to try-out casinos in a couple of villages on the rez. Maybe four or five. Only not in Window Rock, and not right away. So the Vegas bunch gave up when the council wouldn't even see them. Then a couple weeks ago we had another hustler show up to make his pitch, all by himself. He cornered four or five council members, one at a time, about him managing a casino on the rez."

Wince let her vent, leading her through a description of the pressures building in Window Rock. The old lament was familiar, her disappointment with the way the world was turning. Council members were adding up the pros—and ignoring the cons—of following other New Mexico pueblos into the profit of organized gaming.

In Leela's version, that path didn't promise jobs and economic possibilities. It guaranteed disaster. Half the stores in the Window Rock Shopping Center were already boarded up. "A casino on the rez won't open them," she said. "It'll just board up the rest."

Wince nodded. He knew the rumors. New Mexico's casinos, people said, spawned a surge in personal bankruptcies, siphoned off millions of dollars in disposable income, led to mortgage defaults. Small businesses were shaky. Neighborhood restaurants and theaters were closing. And the casinos' revenues did little to help the reservations that housed them. New revenue went out of state. Much of it to Nevada, or to the California or east coast homes of the casino corporation owners. Only the debts stayed in New Mexico. The casinos brought a flood of unanticipated consequences. You could cash the week's paycheck at a casino, blow the family's grocery money on Friday night fun, and head home Saturday morning, broke.

"And we don't need that," Leela said.

"I think you're shouting into the wind. Didn't the Council already approve a casino at Tóhajiilee. That's on Navajo land."

"Tóhajiilee's *off* the rez, an experiment. Like a test case."

"The Council can say 'no.' Didn't they turn down your request for a school computer lab."

"They said no...to *me*. They should say it to those hustlers. Those guys're big-city slick, and some council members are listening. It's plain greed!" She pushed away her flan.

"Did I tell you, one of them called me?" Wince braced for her reaction.

"What do you mean, *called* you?"

"Phone call, yesterday. He said he'd like to meet, next time he's in Albuquerque."

"Called you...before you asked me to lunch? Or after."

"What?" There she was, doing it again.

"Why'd he call *you*?"

"Hey now. It was your brother who gave him my name."

"Rolan? Well, who was the guy?"

"'David' something. Maybe he's not one of the men you talked about."

"*Damnit!*"

"C'mon, Leela" He took her hand, but she jerked free. "He's shopping around. If they find some other place they like better, they'll forget about Window Rock."

"How likely is that?"

Wince shrugged. "When they come around again, introduce me."

"For what?"

"I'd like to meet a high-roller. And maybe I could help."

"The tram's here," she said. "I'm getting a headache." She pushed back from the table and overturned her chair. It crashed to the floor, drawing stares.

As quick as that, the day was over. It was useless to argue with her. Wince pulled her chair upright and waved his Visa card to beckon the waitress. He watched Leela stride from the restaurant to stand at the platform railing outside, her arms folded and fists clenched. Staring west.

When he joined her, Leela marched ahead of him into the tramcar without a word, shoulders stiff, eyes straight ahead.

Other passengers on the flight oohed and aahed over the long view of the city and the west mesa, pointing out the copper glint of the Rio Grande S-turning below them. Wince watched blonde twins of 16 or 17 step away from their parents and stroke Baca's ego by batting their eyes. They whispered to each other and shared giggling. Baca spent the flight down flirting with them, while Wince endured the chill Leela offered him.

After the tramcar docked and Baca ushered everyone off, Leela and Wince passed the crew's locker room, headed to the Mustang in the parking lot below the stone steps outside. Wince knew they resembled what his father, Dimmie, called "Indian Parade." Dad in front, Mom behind him, the kids strung out in a trailing file, a ten-foot gap between any two of them. The whole group might head in the same direction, at the same slow pace, but they didn't talk or even walk together.

Leela was pissed off at the casinos, not at him, but the silence carried its own message. They formed a two-person parade. She led the way, striding off, while Wince slouched after her a few paces back. Telling her about the call from Vegas had torn it, his second mistake of the day.

A problem, for now. But Wince hoped that phone call might even bring a solution. It was a single piece of the puzzle his imagination had begun to assemble. More like a crazy quilt—take a piece from here, one from there.

One good thing: Chutters had driven off. For now.

$ 4 $

When Files was gone, Tedesco hunched forward and said, "Tell me."

"You know I appreciate your support in all this, Mr. Tedescu. And—"

" 'Appreciate,' nothing! I backed the others off when you said you could recover my funds. Do you have them yet?"

" 'Them' … what?"

"*Funds!* My frigging money!"

Money! The old hunky still drew his two per cent percent of the hard count. It was David who'd lost his one percent of the soft totals. More like half-a-percent, after Mr. Tedescu trimmed the figure to stuff his own pockets.

"Do you have the money?"

"No sir, but I—"

"Then…what prospects?"

"Yes, I have pros—"

"What's the time frame? How long do you expect me to wait? You've had more than a month. If I wasn't a generous man, I'd tack some vig on your loan. The meter's running, Tee Jay."

"Yes sir, I appreciate that, and—"

" 'Appreciation' again? I need the money!" He threw a pen at David. "I want the frigging money!"

The pen bounced off his shoulder. David was caught

between fear and the impulse to laugh at the grotesque tantrum. As he waited for Mr. Tedescu to calm himself, he picked up the pen and laid it on the glass desk.

"I'll have a plan roughed out soon," he said. "I'm working on some people right now to organize it," he said. "Say, two months at the outside...or three." He knew he couldn't find a million dollars in three years, let along three months, but without time to try he was screwed. "You'll get the million... or more." He waited.

Mr. Tedescu examined the ceiling for several seconds. Then he nodded, and said, "The Navajo casino? You're talking about that place in New Mexico? The reservation project?"

"Yes sir."

"That's dead. There's no way you can pull that off."

David smiled. "I can." He felt his shirt sticking to his back and shrugged it free but kept his smile in place. *Now*, he thought. One minute, to convince the hunky. "I found an opening."

"The survey crew that greased the way into Puerto Rico couldn't make a dent in those frigging Indians. You say you can?"

Nodding, David kept his cool. "I've got an 'in' your survey crew didn't. A brother and sister I met," he said. "Their name's Begay. Leela and Rolan Begay. They're related to half the Navajos on the reservation, and I can bring them around.

With them on my side...*our* side...they'll help us with the Council there. Them and their buddy from Albuquerque, a small-time contractor named Something Wince."

Mr. Tedescu squinted. "What kind of name is 'Wince?' What extraction? Is he an Indian too?"

David clasped his hands behind him, standing at parade rest, and told his story. Calm, methodical, he offered it just the way he'd rehearsed. Wince and Rolan Begay had been partners in a scam involving stolen turquoise jewelry, an insurance claim. The real blame landed on a pair of New Mexican lowlifes who'd killed a night watchman...all very complicated.

"To what profit?"

"Wince walked off with a couple hundred thousand he split with Rolan Begay. A real tight friendship. Even before Wince started tapping Begay's sister. So now Wince is their savior, and I'll get him to bring the Indians around."

"You can get over on this Wince?"

David laughed. "He's a gomer from East Armpit, New Mexico. What do you think?"

"Buy him?"

"That's one way to go."

"For how much?"

David took a deep breath. "*Uhh*, I haven't got specifics yet."

"But it will cost, am I right? Cost *me!*"

"Maybe some...start-up funds?"

Mr. Tedescu started nodding, his head bouncing above his scrawny neck like a bobblehead toy, considering the possibility. When he spoke, still nodding, he said, "I admire you, Tee Jay. You Harvard schmucks are all smart. Or book-smart, anyway. Only sometimes you trip over your frigging smarts. So what you do for now, you get over to Window Rock, forget about your wild card guy. Stick with the plain vanilla deal. You say you can bring the Indians around? Do it."

"I can—"

"*Do it!* Make that work, do the numbers, show me I'm getting back my money."

"Yes sir."

"Now, I want to believe you, Tee Jay. I'm the one on your side. I want to see you succeed. The California investors wanted to see you…gone."

"The people who fired me?"

"*I* fired you. They wanted to bury you. That is the reason Artie Files will be right beside you from now on. He may not look it, but he's a frigging pit bull. He'll take care of you."

"Yes sir. But when—"

"Make this work, Tee Jay, or I don't need you anymore. *Nobody* needs you."

$ 5 $

Elliott Chávez and Buck Tsosie were inspecting Wince's newest project, installation of a gift shop in his restaurant, *Half-Off*. Chávez still thought of the building as the moving company storage warehouse it had been three incarnations ago. For the past five years it had been *Dimmie's Half-Off*, Albuquerque's only "Navy Restaurant." In the past month, attacked by Wince's crew, it had transformed again. It still housed a huge, empty, banquet hall in the back, overlooking the four-acre parking lot and the closed truck-stop next door. The kitchen sat dead center of the building. It served both the banquet hall behind it and the restaurant out front.

Dimmie's Half Off had been a downscale imitation Denny's with a New Mexican menu. It featured *fajitas pollos*, green *chile* stew, and *carne adovado*. There was no real bar in the place, but the bi-cultural refrigerator held *Tecate, Corona,* and *Dos Equis* as well as Coors and Bud Light. Now this latest renovation of the place had roughed in the framework of a Native American gift shop in the front third of the restaurant, replacing the booths and cutting the 20-foot Formica-topped counter to ten feet long.

"What do you think Dimmie would say if he saw his restaurant now?" Chávez said. He looked over the rough plans Wince had drawn for his crew.

28

"When he retired, he told Robert to go ahead, do what he wants," Tsosie said.

"You think he meant bring in all this junk?" Chávez waved at the shelves and cases dotted with moccasins and beadwork and *faux*-silver engravings. Not enough to fill the display cases, the scattered goods seemed a sample of what might be. A few pots and bottles of jams and jelly and a rainbow range of salsas, red, to yellow, to green, to black. Cactus candy and arrowheads, turquoise and wooden beads, samples scattered here and there. A single pair of bookends fashioned from slices of petrified wood. There were three sand paintings and a few tin bookmarks, leather chaps, a hat rack that held a pair of Resistols and a Stetson. There were bridles and spurs and even a battered old mule pack saddle hung on display near the door.

Tsosie scanned their handiwork and said "No. But Robert had this idea…"

"Yeah, I know his ideas. One of them got him couple years of state time in Santa Fe. Right now the motel comes first. Then he can screw around with this place. Dimmie shouldn't have dumped it on him. Bob's juggling a dozen different… Oh, the hell with it. I guess he'll work it out. —You suggest this gift shop thing to him?"

"He's the one full of ideas. Not me."

"You didn't say 'no.'"

Tsosie shrugged. "He put my name on the window." Tsosie reached out to tap the glass where his name glistened in gold letters. "*Tsosie's Gifts.*" Poised that way—his hair clubbed in a stub braid, beaded turquoise wristband but no watch—he might have been a poster for a John Wayne movie. "When someone offers you a partnership for no cash, for nothing but sweat equity, what do you do?"

"I'd ask him what the hell he's up to." Chávez waved at the waitress polishing glasses behind the abbreviated counter. "Janie? Could I get some of that coffee? To go."

She stood behind the truncated Formica-topped counter, only five stools long, now. She looked at the pair of Pyrex pitchers on the warming burners, one of them empty, and said, "Decaf's all I got. Okay?"

"*Ahhh...* I guess." Chávez turned a questioning look to Tsosie.

"Nothing."

Chávez rolled up the planning sketches. He slipped them into an aluminum tube and capped the end. "I got two men out sick, and we're a week behind schedule. When Bob gets back here, tell him to keep his cell on, okay? Unless you want to make decisions for him."

"Not me," Tsosie said. "He's the man. I'm just the hired help, the token Indi'n. Janie's going to run the lunch counter, serve people her watery coffee. I'll be selling all these authentic Indi'n souvenirs we get from Hong Kong."

"And charm them," Janie said to Tsosie, handing Chávez a styrofoam cup. "You got this famous Indian charm, people say. Celebrity story-teller. Far as I'm concerned, you can start up your charm any time you want. Don't wait for the tourists to get here.

"Oh, Elliott," she said. "Tell Bob his cop friend's been back again. The good looking guy. Dan Chutters. Just hanging around, I don't know why."

"Jesus! What's he want? The place isn't even open yet!"

Chávez slammed the tube against his palm. "I got to get to work."

Wince parked on Los Arboles in Old Town and watched Leela walk into her brother's shop. At least she turned and smiled before she disappeared inside.

Begay's Indian Arts was housed in a small adobe home in Albuquerque's Old Town, one of Wince's first solo remodeling projects. He still considered it his finest work. He wished he could do it over, just for the enjoyment. Adobe walls, hand-hewn, fitted door- and window-frames, restored pine *vigas* projecting out over the slate walk that led from the store to the street…a display of craftsmanship and affection for New Mexico traditions. Once matched by the similar home that shared this cottonwood-shaded double lot, Begay's Indian Arts now outshone it. The new owners of the house next door had ruined it for Wince. They'd painted the window frames pink. *Pink!*

"They're your neighbors. You talk to them about that?" Wince asked Rolan Begay. The two stood on the *portal* fronting Begay's Indian Arts.

"And say what? 'You stupid *gringos*, why're you screwing up Wince's model home?' Like that?"

"Not those words, maybe, but you could let them know pink's not right."

"They own the house now. The Golden Rule says if they got the gold, they make the rules," Begay said. "Is Leela heading home?" He pointed toward the apartment Leela had vanished into, in the back of his gift shop. "Or is she staying here?"

"You know her better than I do."

"Oh-oh. You two have a fight?"

"Let it go," Wince said. "I'm going out to the site to see how Elliott's doing."

Rolan beckoned. He pointed at the display cases. "What do you think?"

"Did you change it?" Wince bent over and scanned the display of turquoise and silver spread on a blue velvet cloth. A spread of antique pieces, bracelets and *jacla* and *heishi* strands and squash blossoms. He spotted the turquoise *jacla* whose replica Rolan always wore, a soft blue collar. Advertising his shop's collection. Wince said, "It looks the same to me."

"I put in new lights. A little pink in them, warms the whole case. See?"

"*Pink?!*"

"Relax, Bob.—Can I get you some coffee?"

"No time," Wince said.

Rolan stepped between Wince and the doorway, blocking his path. "At least stay long enough to listen." He tugged his shirt loose at the waist and took a breath. "You've got to slow down, Robert. The restaurant's tough enough. Now this motel…. You're running yourself ragged."

"You don't get it, man. A construction job's like a good meal. The chef's got to time everything right down to the minute. The salad should be cold and crisp, potatoes done right, steak medium rare, beans cooked firm and not mushy. Every dish has to start cooking at a different time, if they're all gonna hit the table at once."

"Your fancy dinners all come with beans?"

"*Abichuelas*, not *frijoles*."

"Quit hiding behind your Spanish. You do that any time you can't answer."

"C'mon, Rolan. I'm juggling a dozen schedules. Walls and framing have to wait till the plumbing's in. Then wiring gets pulled and insulation blown in or stapled before slapping up drywall, while the painters stand around playing with themselves. A crew isn't a team. It's more like a dozen different workers on separate jobs, each one bitching that somebody else is delaying them. When you're ready for drywall you discover your two drywall guys got hired by American Homes, or Bradbury, or some other big guys."

"Hold it! Take a breath! So if the motel project's got you chasing your own tail, why re-do your restaurant at the same time?"

"Remodeling *Half-Off*'s going to save my neck, just by keeping the crew working. One day Elliott and I'll be big enough to keep a crew fulltime. No down-time when somebody walks away. Nobody taking a job in Santa Fe just when I need him here.

"We'll have a spec house somewhere in town to work on when there's down-time for them at the main job. No worrying about losing a good carpenter; if you can send him to work on the spec house for two or three days. Whatever's blocking him on the main job gets finished, he can come back to work. He keeps getting a check, we keep him busy enough to stay with us. That's why I sent a couple men over to the restaurant to rip out some booths and rough in the gift shop. Losing them or replacing them, that'd cost me more in the long run than paying them to do make-work."

Begay shook his head. "You're so busy, you decide to take on another project. Hell of a solution. You got yourself into a spiral, Bob. Down and down and down."

"Yeah, well, it's my spiral." Wince trotted toward the street. "Tell Leela I'll call."

$ **6** $

Wince drove out Lomas to the motel construction site, mulling over the snarl he was creating for himself with yet another project. No one he could tell about it, until the pieces fell into place. Not Leela, not Elliott...no one. He had the components of the shaky arch he was building. Now, if he could keep the tottering structure standing till the Vegas guys, headed his way, handed him the keystone....

Till then he had a living to make, and a score of people depending on him, Chávez and their crew among them.

"Where's Leela?" Chávez scrubbed a palm over the sun-burned bald spot in his buzz cut. He peered at Wince's Mustang parked at the curb.

"She's staying at Rolan's place," Wince said.

"You and Leela having trouble?" Chávez sat on the dropped tailgate of his Ram pickup, sorting through a sheaf of bills. Wince knew most were routine. A few were overdue. And three of the biggest, from the Sandia Collection Agency, were nearing sheriff's demand. A process-server's visit short of a judgment that could shut down the job.

"The Tribal Council's meeting this week, and she wants to be there. She's going home tonight."

"She riding up there with Buck? —I know. It's none of my business, but... Okay, let it go, sorry I asked. You want me

35

to pay these?" Chávez waved the three collection-agency invoices he held.

"I'm getting sick of dodging the phone calls, so I guess we'd better. But don't bounce any checks. Pay just those three. We'll stall the rest until Garcia brings a check to settlement,"

They were parked on Lomas near Tramway Boulevard, outside the former Eastside Motel. The motel's rusted tin sign lay dented beside the temporary cyclone fence surrounding the construction site. The site had a new sign, a plywood billboard that read:

Sunrise Plaza—Retail Locations Available
Sunrise Apartments
Wince-Chávez Construction.

The motel had been empty for six months when Wince found it. Flushed with success because they had remodeled and flipped four single-family dwellings in the past year, Wince and Chávez had tripled the size of their crew to take on the resurrection of the Eastside Motel. Their biggest project to date. In effect, a gamble…without visiting a casino.

Wince took a deep breath, took a deeper mortgage, and bought the place. A construction an at prime-plus-three paid for the remodeling.

Or should have. But in fact his checkbook was starting to bleed.

After a three-month reconstruction blitz, they had transformed the 60-room motel into 10 four-room apartments and eight retail shops. Construction was near completion, the final decorating getting there, but at almost $14,000 over budget and a week late. So far. After they finished the drywall in number four, the job would be all paint brushes, spackle and glazing. No more hammers. Wince and Chávez were both ready to start smiling. Ready, but not yet able.

"We'll wrap it up in like maybe two weeks," Chávez said, "Ten days, if I can keep Stapely and Ordaz from killing each other."

"Now what?"

"Stapely can't finish framing number four till Ordaz gets the vent and soil pipe in, and replacing the old cracked ceramics with PVC takes time. It's a day-by-day thing. Gripes all the time. Same old shit, you know how it goes. One argument short of banging heads."

"Maybe if we paid them off…"

"Paying them's not enough. If we kill one of them, the other one might quit bitching and do a day's work."

"Ordaz can't be that tough to handle," Wince said. "He's always—"

"*Creo que si.* Except, Wheezer saw him stick a potato up Stapely's tailpipe, and when—"

"A potato?"

Chávez laughed. "No shit, a little potato. You know, block the tailpipe, screw up the compression, and it kills the engine."

"An onion works too."

"You want me to dump 'em both?" Chávez waited for an answer.

"Not for two weeks. After they finish up."

"It's not about money, is it?" Wince said. "I appreciate everyone's patience on wages. You too."

"Skip it. They're okay, except they hate each other. But we could lose Sandoval or maybe Packard if we don't—"

"Keep the crew paid. The suppliers can wait
They get a one-point-five bump every month we're late."

"How long can you stall them?"

"I'm working on something."

"What? Did you sell another unit?"

"No, it's just…call it a windfall I found."

"That means a hustle, right? You got some thing going. ¿Quieres a dime?"

"When the time's right."

"Ayyyy! One of those, huh?…. OK, don't tell me. — Is there any thing you need me to do?"

"Uh-unh. Let's take a walk." The night air was ripe with the loamy scent of new-laid sod. Wince dropped off the tailgate and led his partner through the entry archway and out back between the two wings of the U-shaped building. Three apartments up, two down, on each side. Five retail spaces spaced across the front of the building, were already rented. The ten apartments reached to the rear in parallel, two-story wings overlooking a central courtyard. Retailand residential together, a mom and pop design. A 20-space, asphalt-paved parking lot reached to the alley beyond a crepe myrtle hedge.

The Sunrise Plaza project required a full crew. Crew boss Gene Sandoval had supervised the sub-contractors on the paving and cement work. Skinny Larry Gonzalez was the crew's journeyman electrician. He'd lost 11 pounds he couldn't spare in three months of ten hour days, harrying the pair of apprentices whose work he double-checked, and some times had to do over when they claimed to be finished.

Clay Stapely did framing and carpentry work and bitched every day about Ordaz's plumbers, whose dawdling slowed him down. The Bosco brothers did the painting.

"Just the three of them?"

"Charlene helped some, and her oldest boy, the kid with the Mohawk. They're real fast and probably better than Mikey. At least they clean up when they're done."

"Call Charlene and the boy. We'll let the two of them finish up number four."

They spent an hour of fading daylight going from one unit to another, checking the crown moldings for corner mortise seams, the seating of light fixtures, plumbing and sprinkler system, the fit on kitchen cabinet doors. Quality testing every bit of the work.

When they'd finished all but number four—still not buttoned up—Wince said, "I'd live here."

"*Bueno.*"

"I'd rather have adobe, and oak or cherry cabinets, but I could live here. And that hedge you've got screening off the parking lot…nice idea."

"Thanks."

"Want to grab a beer?"

Chávez shook his head. "*Creo que no.* My ass is dragging."

Wince said, "Maybe we could stop by *Half-Off* and check it out."

"Hey, Bobby. Let's focus here, okay? Let the restaurant slide, or call that wannabe Mexican who wanted to buy the place, Tom Jones."

"The poor guy calls himself 'Toe-MAS HO-nace.'"

"Like tricky pronunciation's going to prove he's Chicano."

"And yeah, he wanted to *own* the restaurant," Wince said. "But he doesn't really want to *buy* it. My dad would burn it down rather than sell to that *bobo*."

Wince turned to walk back to his Mustang. "Get the crew started in the morning, I may be late. I've got to give Buck a hand."

$ **7** $

"**Where do you want these slots?**" Rolan Begay asked. He had backed in through the restaurant's glass front-door, dragging a hand-cart at a stiff arm's length away from his suit coat. He turned and propped the handcart upright, a pair of wooden crates teetering on it. He dusted nothing off his sleeve.

"Thanks," Wince said, "Anywhere. Open the crates and just leave the slots out." He pointed at the padded *bancos* along the foyer wall, the diners' waiting area. He tossed a claw hammer underhand to Rolan. While Rolan pried loose the metal strapping around the crates and the one-by-three pine boards framing the slots, Wince reached into the open cardboard carton at his feet. He laid a trail of cactus-shaped ashtrays atop the glass display case.

Rolan put the gleaming slot machines on the floor "What's all that crap there?"

"Half this stuff came from your suppliers," Wince said. "Most of it is—"

"Not that plastic trash." Rolan scanned the cluttered room, a former lunch counter now bracketed by display shelves and glass cases. He squinted. "Looks like a Family Dollar Store exploded in here. You and Buck tell me you want to open a gift shop, so I said I'd help. Like you were a branch of my

41

place, you said. But I thought you meant quality goods—silver, turquoise, handwork."

"Hey, Rolan. How are you?" Buck Tsosie entered from the storeroom in the back, carrying an armload of Navajo-pattered blankets—Two Grey Hills. Storm Pattern, Ganado Wool. He began to hang them, one blanket draped dangling over each rung of a rough ladder fashioned from peeled aspen poles. It was a display of fabrics like a geometric water-fall of traditional Navajo colors, crimson, black, white.

Wince nudged the empty carton aside with his foot. "You don't want Buck competing with you. You sell quality. Buck can do affordable. Let him peddle the gimcrackery that tourists buy."

"You say 'Let Buck do it,'" Rolan said. "Aren't the two of you both in this?"

Wince shook his head. No sense arguing with Rolan. He'd burn out soon enough.

Their rare disagreements might smolder but never reached ignition. The two had been friends since their freshman accounting class at the University of New Mexico. But Wince dropped out the next year to take a construction job. Rolan stayed to graduate and parlayed his education and family connections on the Navajo reservation into the ownership of Begay's Indian Arts in Albuquerque's Old Town. That reunited them. Wince remodeled an adobe shell in Old Town into Rolan's apartment-*cum*-showroom. And together they'd profited from a fabulous collection of Navajo turquoise jewelry Rolan claimed he'd discovered on the reservation. He brought to his shop...to be displayed in cases designed and built by Wince.

Rolan's sister Leela was another link between them.

"Buck? You're okay with all this?" Rolan asked. "The truck drivers who used to come in for Dimmie's coffee won't be back for silver collar points or a blanket. Someone who orders a burger doesn't want a plastic turquoise watchband on the side."

"They do at The Cracker Barrel," Wince said. "Or at all the Giant truck stops, or over at Stuckey's."

"C'mon, Bob. Why take the risk? ... Buck? Are you okay with all this?"

Tsosie smiled. "Happy times, all around," he said to Rolan. "I hear you joined the Chamber of Commerce. You're wearing a suit and a red necktie, like a TV guy, and you drive a Lincoln. I think you're already where you want to go. Maybe we're headed a different way, us simple folks."

"Yeah, 'simple.' Bob's running his own fifteen-man crew. This place is something like five acres of pricey real estate he ought to sell—"

"Find me a buyer," Wince said.

"Great location. You're sitting on property worth better than four or five hundred kay, I'd guess. So don't give me any of your 'blue collar' crap. You're only two or three jobs away from going big time, if you stay with what you know. Instead of always trying something new."

"Come back in a couple weeks and see what we do with this place."

"I thought you wanted to talk business. What you want is an adventure. "You know what kind of trouble those slots are?" Rolan nudged one of the slot machines with his foot. "What do you need 'em for? You going to run them?"

"Leave them right there. They're a display."

"You see what happened to the old supermarket over on Central? They had slots in the place, selling them, and got caught. They paid a *big* fine. Like maybe twenty-five thousand dollars. You can't sell slots. Not ones that pay off, anyway. You damn sure can't run them, unless you're an Indian casino. Or a service club, like the Lions and, what d'y call 'em, the Elks. … Buck?"

Tsosie shrugged. "Talk to Robert."

"You know those things are trouble, just sitting there."

"Decorations," Wince said. "Someone walks in and sees them here, he'll know what we might make of the place. Ot's called 'potential,' OK?"

"Hey! I'm only looking out for you. For *us*! If you're in trouble again, we're all screwed."

"Not you, just Buck and I. Anyway, those things only look like real slots."

"They're not real?"

"Class two instead of three, something like that. I don't know the difference. This kind's legal, like the old pinball machines, as long as they don't pay off. Winner gets points instead of cash. We'll leave them right here in the shop."

"Where anybody who comes in can trip over them."

"Where anybody can see them."

"I'd hide them back in the store room." Rolan walked out, shaking his head, leaving Tsosie and Wince to organize the scatter of gift items strewn on the floor. More trinkets in crates and cartons and bags. The novelty would surprise the nearby store owners along I-25 who knew *Dimmie's Half-Off* only as a mediocre restaurant.

"Janie? You need some help there?"

"You'd just mess it up," she said, kneeling beside the under-counter cabinets, cleaning the storage spaces as she emptied them. Janie Collier knew where all the serving dishes were stored, soup bowls to butter ramekins, cups and plates and saucers. They were 'hers.' She was the only survivor of the wait-staff who'd worked at *Dimmie's Half-Off* since opening day. And now Wince watched her shuffle through pairs of salt shakers and pepper mills, the clutter of tea pots and tin ware, reducing the number of kitchen supplies to suit the café the former restaurant was becoming. She hooked a thumb at Rolan's stagey exit and rolled her eyes.

"He'll get over it," Wince said. He disconnected the soft drink tanks under the fountain and struggled to pull them out of their under-counter brackets.

Tsosie unpacked and counted miniature *talavera*-faced refrigerator magnets.

The three worked with little conversation, busy with scut work jobs the boss has to do.

$ 8 $

"What's going on, Wince?" Detective Dan Chutters stood in the doorway. "You decide to quit making coffee? Or'd Starbucks get too tough for you?" He wore a wrinkled sport coat and a tie, his new working uniform. No nightstick on his belt, no mace.

"One of Albuquerque's finest asks you for coffee," Wince said, "we'd better find him some,"

Wince said. He waved at Janie.

Tsosie said nothing.

"Skip the coffee," Chutters said. "Just curious."

Wince nodded. "Restaurant's closed till we finish remodeling." He indicated the work underway. "We'll be serving again soon. Say two weeks or so."

Chutters scanned the cluttered room, musing. "I drive by here couple times a day and I saw you were up to something, since Dimmie left. What's going on?'"

"Just trying to make a living."

"Really? You got the world by the tail, I hear. Restaurant mortgage paid down, your dad retired off to somewhere, and…"

"San Diego."

"Is that right? So now, *Dimmie's Half-Off* is all yours, without Dimmie. Maybe you ought to change the name."

"Would that be okay with you?"

46

"Hey now!" Chutters turned to face him.

"There it is, that attitude. For no reason." With the blurted irritation, his Midwestern twang surfaced. After a deep breath, he said. "Don't you tell your friends what you're up to?"

"You and I friends, detective?"

Tsosie leaned against a counter and waited. Janie pretended to polish the creamers she'd assembled on a tray.

"Why not? I admire a real lucky bugger like you," Chutters said. "How many people walk through a shit storm and come out the other side covered with money? A year ago you were up in Santa Fe, doing time. Fraud, wasn't it? Double-billing for one of your construction jobs?"

"A little misunderstanding."

"Your pa's restaurant here was in the toilet. Then, out of nowhere, you and Begay stumble on all that turquoise jewelry."

"Good luck," Wince said.

"Only...the turquoise disappears. *Poof!* Stolen."

"You're the one who solved that, right?"

"Off your tip. Very generous."

"No need to thank me."

"Uh-huh. And *shazam!*" Chutters snapped his fingers. "The insurance company pays off.

That's probably better for you and Begay than selling the stuff. Instant cash, no work involved. Only...I worry about anybody who stumbles into easy money."

Wince smiled. "Like *shazam!* You end up a detective. Overnight easy promotion."

"I earned it!"

"Then…congratulations. … Are we done?"

"For now." Chutters looked around the restaurant again but said only, "I'll be watching to see how far your luck takes you."

"I appreciate the attention."

The silence stretched. Neither mentioned Chutters' trailing him.

Tsosie put a hand on Wince's arm to calm him and said to Chutters, "Thanks for stopping in, Detective. You're always welcome."

"Yeah. Sure, Welcome.'" Chutters swallowed whatever else he wanted to say, waited for a comment from Wince, and then took his time leaving. At the door he said, "Good luck, then. …Only not too good." The door swung shut behind him.

Tsosie motioned for Wince to relax. "There's no point quarreling with 'the man.' If he comes back, let me talk, okay? He doesn't envy me."

Wince peered out the front window, watching Chutters climb into the unmarked, distinctive Crown Vic. "You think that's what it is?"

"Hell yes! I'm somebody he can label. Just a dumb Indi'n, done state time for drinkin' and fightin'. He's got me pegged. But you, he can't figure out yet, and that gnaws at him."

"You think?"

"Cops are puzzle-solvers, and you're a kind of puzzle. For all Chutters knows, you might turn out respectable—make your fortune honest and go middle class, like Rolan."

"You think?"

"No, you like games too much. And Chutters is a worrier."

"Nothing to worry about, but thanks. — Listen. Will you do me a favor? Are you willing to take a run up to Window Rock tomorrow?"

"That's three hours drive, each way! It's not like going out to pick up some milk." He looked up at the wall-mounted clock.

"Tomorrow, not now. I need you and Rolan to go up and work the Council. Try to get their support for the buying group I told you about. At least plant the idea with them."

"I thought you were gonna negotiate that."

"If I walk into a council meeting...if they'll even let me in...what then? I'm standing bare-faced in front of eighty-some Indians. Who's the council going to listen to? Me, or another *Diné*."

"*Adopted Diné.* I explained it to—"

"That still gives you more connection than I've got. Who could persuade them? Me or you?"

"Neither one of us. ...Rolan, maybe. Or maybe Leela."

"Then use Rolan or Leela. Whichever one's got more credibility."

"So, for that you want me to drive all the way up to Window Rock."

"The council's in session this week. Then not for another three months. ...Right? Once a quarter?"

"They do less damage that way." Tsosie grew sly. "Would you call this a a business trip?"

Wince laughed. "Buck, you're something else. Okay, it's business. You drive, I'll buy the gas. But it's up to you. Either go hustle the council, or come back in here tomorrow and keep unpacking."

Janie looked up from her spot behind the counter. "Woman's work."

Tsosie said, "A no-brainer, Robert. I'll see you." He walked out humming.

Janie got to roll her eyes again. — She said, "What's that mean, 'buying group'?"

"Not a big thing. Just an idea." And one more piece of fabric for the crazy quilt he envisioned. "If we get all the gift shops in the area to buy in a block, like a co-op, we can get better prices. Rolan will go for it, I know. Buck and I already talked it over. You'll see. We'll call it the Begay Inventory Association."

An hour later, the last carton unpacked, Wince asked, "D'you remember Tom Jones? ... Not Tom Jones, the singer. Tom Jones, that lobbyist, used to come in here."

"Toe-MAS HO-nace?" Janie said. "The fake Mexican."

Wince smiled. "That's the guy. I'm surprised he hasn't been sniffing around since my dad left."

Janie craned to look out the window as if searching for someone, hesitating. "He has. I should have told you, except you're so busy, I didn't want you worried about it. He's been here, like out in the parking lot or sitting in his car down the block, maybe six or seven times. Kind of like he was waiting for something. But he never comes in. He used to come around, sucking up to Dimmie. Part of that Hispanic bunch wants to buy *Half Off*."

Wince walked behind the counter and helped himself to a cup of coffee.

"Can I heat that up for you?" Janie said.

"No, it's O.K. ... So if they were eager to buy the place, why do you think they gave up?"

"After what's-her-name went to jail, they're like a snake with the head cut off. Who's their boss now? And don't tell me it's Jones, or HO-nace, or whoever he thinks he is."

Wince drank the tepid coffee and made a face. "*Bleeagh!* Dump this out, okay? We don't hate anyone this much." He handed her the cup. "And if HO-nace comes around again, let me know?"

"I'm sorry I didn't tell you, Bob, really I didn't—"

"Skip it. I thought I didn't want to talk to him. Now, maybe I do."

$ 9 $

On the way west from Albuquerque on I-40, passing Grants, lulled by the regular thump of the tires counting highway expansion joints, Tsosie had decided he needed a morning nap and asked Leela to take the wheel.

The steering of the Ford 150 was tight but she had no trouble with it. Interstate traffic was light, the morning sky clear. She debated turning on the radio but decided to let Buck sleep while she took stock.

Three men in her life. Her brother Rolan was always busy these days, busting his hump for success. Robert was smart, and strong, and quiet, maybe even the prince she'd spent her frog-kissing years looking for…but he wasn't *Diné*. Buck *was Diné*, although 'adopted' *Diné*, he claimed. Three men, all different. Now, if she could only shuffle and reassemble their virtues…

Buck was ready to build their *hogan*, any time she agreed. And he *was Diné*. Robert had surprised her by saying he might move to Window Rock, if she demanded it. As sweet as he was, as much as he obviously cared for her, it probably couldn't work. She knew he'd be miserable within weeks. And Rolan was already lost; he'd given up mutton and frybread and turned to frozen strawberries and the South Beach diet. She smiled. Maybe not 'lost,' but drifting away.

She swung off I-40 and turned north out of Gallup on 461

headed toward 264 and Shiprock. The pickup bounced and rattled crossing the railroad tracks. The rough grade crossing woke Buck.

"They've still got the old signs here," he said.

Leela said, "Welcome back."

"See the signs?"

"I thought you were asleep."

"Now I'm not." He pointed at the antiqued highway sign they were passing, 666, it read, a new signed painted to look old. Just beyond it a newer-looking sign disagreed, labeling the road as 461. "Used to be, someone would ask where you were going on this road, you might say 'Goin' to the devil.' So they changed the name. Only then they kept the old ones too, all painted old style. So now the road's got two names. Or numbers."

"People are funny."

"No, it made sense, changing the name. Always was a lotta accidents along in here. — Six-sixty-six, that's the sign of the devil."

"Buck, you don't believe that stuff."

"I'm just reporting. You want to check it? Give a man a couple of stiff drinks, send him out to drive six-sixty-six."

"Now there won't be any more accidents after the name change?"

"I'm just sayin', some things might be coincidents. Some aren't."

Leela smiled. "You ready to drive?"

"Keep going. You haven't wrecked us yet. I'll drive back down, if you decide to head back to Albuquerque with me."

"We'll see."

At Yahtahhey, more wide spot in the road than village, she took the left fork toward Window Rock. Robert was right, this drive was a pain. It took almost three hours, even at Interstate speeds. And he'd made the trip every weekend for the past few months, or she had. Once they tried meeting in Grants, roughly halfway between her home on the rez and Robert's place in Albuquerque's north valley, but that was worse. Both of them had to drive.

Leela crossed the state line into Arizona and bounced through a pair of welcoming potholes. She didn't like the eastbound ride any better than Robert did, but she always looked forward to this part of the westbound trip. With each mile north out of Gallup the terrain changed from flat to ever more tumbled and hilly until she rounded a banked curve, and 'the haystacks' came into view. Tawny colored, softly mounded sandstone hills south of Window Rock, they promised that home was only minutes away.

"We're here," she said, and watched Buck shake himself and then crack his knuckles, like a piano-man loosening up.

"You headin' over to council chambers?" he asked at the stoplight.

She answered by pointing at the Window Rock Inn. "Rolan said he'd meet us." She turned into the parking lot.

Rolan was waiting at a window-side table in the coffee shop. Someone with a marketing imagination had renamed it to impress. No longer termed a lunch counter, it was now *The Diné Lounge*. "I watched you pull in," Rolan said. "You see they painted The Red Room?"

A door beside the reception desk stood open to reveal a

woman vacuuming the carpet inside the small private dining room. "I guess now it's the Pinky-Orange room," Rolan said.

"Coral." Leela pointed at the wall-mounted sign beside the door—*Yoó ticíí,* "coral," in *Diné.*

"They changed that, couple years ago," Buck said to Rolan. "Been awhile since you been back?" He winked at Leela.

"Yeah, yeah," Rolan said.

Leela nodded. "Rolan and I had our high school graduation parties in the Red Room, both of us. A century ago, for me. Two centuries for him. The whole room was painted red, red woodwork, red wallpaper, red carpet, red and red and red...till they redecorated here. Rolan missed all that. He lives in Albuquerque now and forgot where he came from."

"I remember the red," Rolan said.

"What's it feel like, being back?" Leela said.

"Enough!" Rolan drained his cup. "You two got me up here to do you a favor, you said. What's going on?"

"Besides visiting family...? It's Robert's idea," Tsosie said. "You know all the True Valu Hardware stores? There's something like eight thousand of them, all independent, but they buy together. That's buying power. *Deep* discounts."

"I appreciate the information. What's your point?"

"If we get together all the gift shops on the rez, and at the Fort, maybe all over Arizona and New Mexico, we could buy as a single group. With more clout, more buying power, we could cut costs by what? Ten percent? Twenty? Robert wants us to approach the council and ask their help. Their endorsement of us, putting together the group."

"Us?"

"Okay," Tsosie said. "You."

"I don't have any special 'in' with the council. Why would they back your buyIng group on my say-so?"

"Not Buck's buying group," Leela said. "*Yours*. Rolan Begay, the respected businessman. You own property. You traded your pickup in on a Lincoln. I'll bet you even had to pay taxes last year." She gave him her best smile. "Buck didn't." She beckoned the waitress who was hovering nearby. "You help Buck get his foot in the door, it'll help you too. You, and Buck, and all the gift shops in the Four Corners area. We'll call it the 'Begay Inventory Association.'"

"Where'd that come from?"

"Another of Robert's ideas," Tsosie said.

"Any shop in the Begay Inventory Association will save money. And they'll all be advertising your store, using the association name. It'll be worth it. Membership won't cost them anything. You think they'll turn down the chance to pay less for their goods? I sure wouldn't."

The waitress waited, pencil poised.

"Let's order," Leela said. "We'll eat while you marshal your objections, and I'll tell you why you're wrong."

Rolan flipped open his menu. He nodded but said nothing.

$ **10** $

Artie Files and T. J. David sat parked outside the Navajo Council chambers in Window Rock. The red sandstone council building itself wasn't imposing. One squat story high, octagonal, red and tan, it looked like patchwork architecture, a dozen afterthoughts, slapped onto a tool shed. East of it, beyond a small parking area, temporary wooden buildings housed staff offices. They reminded David of a trailer park, a rank of double-wides. Capitol of the Navajo Nation. A trailer park dwarfed by the two-hundred-foot sandstone ridge at the end of the street. The ridge was a sharp-spiked dusty spine thrown up against the morning sun. It was pierced by a circular hole that named the village. Window Rock.

David fidgeted in the back seat of the rented stretch Lincoln and scanned the brochure he'd picked up at the Navajo Service Administration building. Navajos had long ago named the place *Tséghánoodzán* or Perforated Rock. David snorted. Pretentious name. Near the window itself was a spring that provided medicine men with water for *Tóhee*, the Water Way Ceremony. Maybe interesting, if you were an Indian, or thirsty.

David tossed the brochure to the jump seat beside him and leaned back to stretch his legs. Over four hundred miles on the road. He would have chartered a plane, but there was no chance Mr. Tedesco would pay for it, so he'd had little choice.

Even in the Lincoln, the best Files had been able to hire, the ride down from Vegas had been hot and tiring. You'd think at $65 a day, the lousy air conditioning would work.

Overnight in Gallup and the wait here on this grubby little street with Files for company was increasing his irritation. David leaned forward and said. "Radio. A classical station."

Nodding, Artie Filed snapped on the radio.

"Did you hear me?"

"What do you think I'm doing?" He punched in 'seek.'

"Then answer me!"

Files nodded.

His "driver," David told himself. Wonderful! Dumb muscle, incapable of a civil conversation, Files must have doused himself in Old Spice, one more irritant on a day, in a week, filled with them. David stretched his legs and seized both trouser knees, pinching the creases and tugging loose the linen stranglehold on his crotch. "Classical station, I said."

Files looked over his shoulder. "I could stick in a CD, if you got one. We're out here a hundred miles from the world. No reception in this fuckin' dust bowl you got me parked in. Radio don't come through rock mountains, you know. We get out of here, then I'll get you your classic music. Meanwhile, what are we waiting for? The Indians won't let you go in there, you said. Into the council building. So why sit here?"

"Do you have somewhere to go? Some pressing engagement?"

Files shrugged and watched the radio LED display flicker as the seek function stepped its abrupt way from one station to another, guitars all the way, acoustic to steel to rock to country to static.

After ten minutes, the Council Chamber double doors split open to emit a parade.

"There!" David said. "Council's out. There they come!"

Two men in jeans and sweaters led the way, followed by three others just as casually dressed, then a man in a sport coat and a short, heavy man in a brown suit, a woman on his arm. Malcolm Obee.

"That one!" David said. "The chubby man and woman."

The couple crossed to a Chevy van parked under a cottonwood across the street.

"They're going to lunch somewhere. Follow them."

Files looked back again. "There's only three or four restaurants in the whole town. Where can they—?"

"Follow them!"

Muttering under his breath, Files trailed the van less that a quarter mile to the Window Rock Inn and pulled into an empty parking space.

David watched the pair walk on ahead into the coffee shop. The large lot was filling as a lunch crowd assembled. "I'll be back," he said, getting out of the car.

"Me too." Files opened the driver's door. "I ain't had my lunch yet," he said. "And I'm not starving in the fuckin' car while you eat."

The coffee shop was nearly full. David bypassed the queue at the hostess' stand and took a seat, not far from Obee and his companion.

The hostess hurried to David's table. "Sir? We have others waiting."

"They won't have to wait long," he said. "Those four kids there are leaving."

"Which...?" She turned to look.

"Over by the window." David pointed and waved her away. "And get me a menu."

She hesitated, stood still, uncertain. Then she surrendered and handed each of them a menu. She hurried back to her lectern.

Files tapped the corner of the menu against his teeth, watching the hostess cross the room. When she spoke to the three men at the head of the queue, he said. "Okay. So let's do it. They got anything here a white man can eat?"

They spent thirty minutes at the table, Files slurping his spaghetti. David turned away in disgust and kept an eye on Malcolm Obee and the woman with him. She looked Indian. Brunette, about thirty, tight skirt and sweater, Reeboks tapping as she kept time with the hokey disco music that pulsed through the coffee shop.

But it was Obee that David focused on. A lobbyist, David had learned. For hire. Someone with negotiable principles, and a possible advocate with the council. Their entrée.

Files eyed the woman. "Good rack," he said.

David pushed his cup away. "I'll be back." He rose and crossed the room.

"That's the one," Leela said. "The one talking to Malcolm." She cocked her head toward David and Obee without looking their way.

"No big deal," Rolan said.

"It is!" Leela said. "You know he's recruiting, looking for some hired gun to plead his case with the council, and—"

"Kind of like you want me to intercede with the Council about the buying group."

"Exactly like that," Tsosie said. "Except, you know, we're the good guys."

"And you know he wants to manage a casino here on the rez. Him with his blowing smoke, his big talk about Vegas connections. He can make us rich. He knows the right people."

"Okay, all right, Leela. Let it go," Rolan said. "It hasn't happened yet. And the guy can't turn the council around by himself. Just relax."

She leaned back in her chair, nodding. "Maybe. ...But do you want to see Window Rock owned by those gangsters? Because that's what it'll come to."

"Be calm," Rolan said. "Don't cry till you're hurt." He turned to Tsosie. "Am I right, Buck?"

"About money, usually. This time it's about people, so I don't know."

Leela watched the conversation at Obee's table. Obee introduced his wife, Sharon, to the two men. One was tall and wearing a tan linen suit, the other a smirking jock in a shiny warmup suit and gold chains. She named them to herself: 'Slick' and 'the Chimp.' She saw the Chimp slide a chair closer and sit down beside Sharon. Slick and Obee turned to walk toward her. They stopped beside the table.

"Hey, Rolan. How are you?" Obee reached out to shake hands. "Hello Buck," he said. "Good to see you. And Leela. This is Tee Jay David. He's a visitor here, his second time in Window Rock."

David said, "My pleasure," nodding to them.

"Second time?" Buck said. "You leave something here the first time?"

Rolan said, "Welcome back."

The three men looked at Leela. And waited.

With a broad smile and deep sincerity, she said, *"yiníyáhídę́ę́'góó naadááł. doo naanideestseel da nisin."*

"Leela!" Rolan flinched and motioned Lela quiet, patting the air. Buck covered his smile.

"I beg your pardon?" David said. "I'm not very good with languages." He smiled…waiting.

"Rolan," she said. *"áta' hólne' daats'í?"*

It was Obee who jumped in. "Thank you, Leela. Right. Okay. Good to see you." He clapped an arm around David's shoulders and said, "Let's go have that talk."

The pair walked off.

"Good!" Leela nodded. "Take him outside and *yóó'anílt'e.*"

"C'mon, Leela!" Rolan glared at her. "What if he understands *Diné*?"

"Fat chance!"

$ **11** $

Wince ushered Leon Quintana into the empty banquet room behind the new gift shop and handed him a cold *Tecate* longneck. "What did you find out?"

"I went over to the Law School library and went online with *LexisNexis*, *Westlaw* and the *Codex Mexicana*. Spent nearly two hours."

"At how much an hour?"

"Hey, man. Just a favor. My meter's not running yet, not till you give me more guidance on this."

Wince nodded his thanks. More than his attorney, Quintana was a jogging partner who'd once talked him into sky diving, and then…almost a logical next step…base jumping…a burst of folly he'd abandoned after three jumps. Jogging was okay, if a waste of time. He even worked up a sweat on Quintana's stair climber. And base jumping from a hot air balloon was okay. Kind of a cool. But no more jumping off a rocky cliff-face into the wind.

Quintana had handled the purchase of the property and had drawn up a file folder full of sales agreements, and was ready to go to settlement with the five buyers already lined up to take possession of the retail units when construction was complete. He and Wince were both waiting to be paid by the buyers. It couldn't happen too soon.

The two picked their way through a scatter of styrofoam

63

peanuts and bubblewrap crackling underfoot on the banquet hall floor. Folded chairs lay stacked against the rear wall. Cases of *Tecate* empties blocked the door into the alley. A metal bookcase beside them held packs of napkins, cases of toilet paper, two rolls of brown butcher paper. The room echoed their footsteps. It smelled of beer, bleach and floor wax.

"Big room," Quintana said. "You need all this storage space?" He tipped his head back and drank half his *Tecate*.

"Wait and see," Wince told him. "Have you found out about Buck Tsosie's people? Can we prove his lineage?"

"The Bureau of Indian Affairs lists six hundred fifty two registered tribes, pueblos, and sites, villages, and organizations…names I never heard of. But no *Tlaxcalans*."

Wince sat on an empty display case. "Can you work them onto the list? I know two state legislators who owe me, only I don't think they've got much clout outside of Santa Fe."

"No, we don't want to do this piecemeal. My idea is, we apply for a declaration of reciprocity. A colleague in Juarez says the Mexican government grandfathered the *Tlaxcalans* onto their approved list, twenty, maybe thirty years ago. So if we can get the Feds to extend blanket recognition to all the tribes already recognized in Mexico, it'll be like a class action. We'd have hundreds of allies to join us, not only *Tlaxcalans*… if we could find any. Will that content Tsosie?"

"He doesn't need the approval. I need it for him."

"What's going on?" Quintana thumbed foam off his lush moustache.

"We're opening an Indian gift shop. The site and owner should be BIA-registered *Tlaxcalans* aren't…yet."

"It'll be complicated."

"You handled the parking lot purchase. That was complicated. And the motel."

"Real estate's a helluva lot easier than dealing with the Feds. Especially is we're going after an international agreement. We might need a Mexican lawyer on this."

"*Tu eres mexicano, ¿verdad?*"

"Not in the Court's eyes. I'm still Chicano, for whatever that's worth, but not Mexican. When my folks moved us up from Chihuahua, we got an instant promotion. From wetback, to *gringo*."

"You'll figure a way. We share reciprocity with Canada on some things, and Mexico."

Quintana finished his beer and looked around for a place to stash the empty.

"Toss it in the barrel there," Wince said. "Can't we wave NAFTA at the feds?"

"We're not after free trade. And there's a basic principle in dealing with government agencies. The less important the issue is, the less some bureaucrat wants to risk his job over it. Only a rookie will take on some piddly-ass deal. Especially something brand new. They all hate any problem that hasn't already been solved a dozen times."

"Precedent, you mean."

"Lawyers' favorite word—'precedent.' Besides that, the Feds will want to know why you care about some extinct Mexican Indian tribe."

"Obscure, maybe. But *Tlaxcalans* are *not* extinct. That's the point."

"Okay, *I* want to know why you care, before we get much

deeper into this." He handed Wince the empty.

Wince reached into the pocket of his Levis and drew out a folded piece of paper. "You know Buck Tsosie."

"Sure. Your new partner, the older guy."

"Older? He's only maybe thirty-five."

"Looks older. ... Rough life?"

"He did some time, less than a nickel. He's a friend of Rolan and Leela."

"Rolan's friend, maybe, but maybe more than friend to Leela."

"You can't blame him…or anyway, I can't."

"All the movie Indians I see are tight-lipped stoics. But Tsosie can't stop yakking. Thinks he's Aesop or Mother Goose. I never heard him answer a question in less than two minutes. He tells stories, just to hear himself talk."

"He'd been telling me a story about family history," Wince said.

"Long one, I'll bet."

"He's full of really good details, only I didn't believe most of his story, until maybe a couple of weeks ago. I drove him up to Santa Fe to pick up his truck from the paint shop, and he showed me about his family. In Santa Fe…."

The church of San Miguel dominates the corner of Vargas and the Old Santa Fe Trail and stands across Vargas from the oldest house in America. Historians say there's been a structure on that site since 1600. And Wince had heard that San Miguel was the oldest original church building in the U.S., built a generation before the pilgrims landed at Plymouth Rock.

"There it is," Tsosie said. "Take a look at that."

Wince read the engraved historic marker outside the church entrance.

Welcome to San Miguel Church. Under the auspices of Fray Alonzo de Benevidas, OFM, this church was built by Tlaxcalan Indians from Mexico in the early 1600s.

"Enough," Tsosie said. "The rest is history of its remodeling. Boring. This roof repair, that paint job, you know. Skip it. Now look at this." He unfolded a wad of stained silk, flipping back the corners to unwrap a thick, leather disk, resting on his palm. He handed it to Wince.

"What is it?" Wince turned it over, untangling the rawhide strap wrapped around it. On one side of the disk was a faint crucifix incised in the stained leather, above the phrase *Deo Gratia*. On the other side...the initials *A.d'B.* He handed it back to Tsosie. "What's it mean?"

"I took it to a professor, a forensic anthropologist at the Maxwell Museum, and it made his day," Tsosie said. "He looked at it, and rubbed it, and started pacing around his office. Almost dancing, he was so pumped. I thought he was going to wet himself. Nobody knows how many of these were made, he said, but two others just like it have turned up. One in the Historical Museum here in Santa Fe. The other's in some church in San Luis Potosi, Mexico. Just like this one. The professor had never seen one up close. They were awards, he said. A kind of recognition for the *Tlaxcalans* who worked on San Miguel. He wanted me to donate it to the Maxwell Museum."

"You didn't."

Tsosie only looked at him.

"How did you get it?"

"In a bag filled with white sand. You know, powdery stuff, like talcum." He took back the medallion and re-wrapped it in the square of stained silk. "My great grandfather left it. Or great-great-great. I don't know how many 'greats' it was. Passed down from oldest son to oldest son. It's been in my family forever." Tsosie stuffed the wrapped medallion into his pocket.

"How long is forever?" Wince said. "The anthropologist tell you that? Leather probably won't last four hundred years."

"It will, if air can't get at it. Packed in talcum sand, it was like in a vacuum bag. And it did last, you know." He tapped his pocket. "It's here, isn't it?"

"I just meant, scientists could test it and tell you its age."

"Uh-huh. And they'd test it by slicing off a piece and dunking it in acid. Or using x-rays. Or burning it and ana-lyzing the ashes. Who knows what else? And maybe destroy a memory left for me to take care of. Well, skip that! Maybe it's worth nothing in dollars, but a whole lot in memories. It's a family heirloom. I can hold it and wonder how many of my people touched it, over the years. It might be an ances-tor of mine earned the medal for helping build this place." He waved at the ocher stucco structure beside them. "Maybe it was part of his wages, maybe a token thank you from de Benavides. Or The Church."

"Hang onto it. For proof."

"Yeah, but the medal, or whatever you call it, isn't the only proof. I told you my family has lived with the *Diné* for generations, without being *Diné* ourselves. ... D'you know about clans?"

"The ancestry thing? A little," Wince said.

"Clans are like family names to your people. A Navajo baby is born *into* the mother's clan, but *for* the father's clan. So when you meet a Navajo...or *Diné*...he'll tell you both his mother's clan and his father's. Someone whose mother was 'tobacco people clan' and whose father was 'turkey people' will tell you he's 'tobacco / turkey.' But he considers himself tobacco people. So will his kids. And especially his daughter's kids.

"But me, I'm nothing. My father's people were *Naakaii Diné*, an adopted clan name that really means 'Mexican people' in *Diné*. But my mother was nobody. She was called 'church builder,' and that's not a clan, just a nickname. So I grew up thinking I was church builder-*Naakaii*. Kind of a half-breed."

"Like I'm Filipino on my mother's side, and 'Wince' on my dad's."

"I didn't know that. ... You're half Filipino?"

"It never meant much to me, except I tan pretty easy."

"At least you *know*. For me it's been weird, not having a clan. I was the only kid I knew who didn't have one. Any time I had to introduce myself, I couldn't say 'Mud People,' or 'Corn People.' I said my mother's people were 'church-builders,' and the other kids giggled like...I don't know. No one said anything about it, but they thought it was funny. They all did."

"All of them?"

"Yeah, me too. And I never put the nickname together

with the totem in the bag of sand. This," Tsosie said, taking out the medallion again. "I never connected the nickname and this...till I saw the sign here. It turns out I may be *Tlaxcalan*. I know I'm not *Diné*. What do you think?"

"Well, what did you think?" Quintana said.

Wince shrugged. "Good story, if it's true...even if it isn't."

"So that's why you're curious about *Tlaxcalans*?" Quintana said.

Wince showed him the slip of paper. "I copied this off a plaque at the church. Buck didn't invent the story."

After reading Wince's notes, Quintana said, "Not all of it, anyway. So what?"

"Maybe we can do something about it. Help him out."

Quintana looked at him. "To prove he's ... whatever."

"*Tlaxcalan*. Because there's no *Tlaxcalan* reservation or facility in the US. If *Tlaxcalans* get BIA recognition, Buck, and any property he owns, automatically gets it too. And a BIA recognized tribe member gets benefits you and I don't."

"That's it?"

"And we might learn something, something profitable."

"Got another beer?" Quintana shook his head. "It's up to you, but it's going to take time, and effort, and even if you can do something for Tsosie, it's going to cost. Time, more than money.—Sunrise Plaza's not paying off yet. I know you're stretched pretty thin, and you've got even less time than money. If it was me, my curiosity doesn't run that deep. D'you *owe* Tsosie for some reason?"

"It's like untangling snarled string. It's got to be done."

"Not by everybody. Lots of people can live with snarled string."

Wince shrugged.

"But not you. So you'll prove he's *Tlaxcalan*. And then...?"

"Everybody needs a family name." Wince led the way back into the kitchen and the walk-in cooler. "Finding him one could be fun."

"Now we're going to all this trouble for *fun*?"

Quintana took the sweating *Tecate* bottle that Wince handed him and shook his head. "I know you better than that. 'Fun,' and what else?"

"You ever hear of salting a mine?"

"What?"

"It's the way to imply what might be." Wince laughed at himself. "Skip it. It's a long story."

"Yours? Or Buck's?" Quintana said.

Wince smiled. Another piece of the crazy quilt he was stitching together.

$ 12 $

Back in the Lincoln, T.J. David leaned forward and snapped his fingers to get Files's attention. "Close the window," he said.

Files made eye contact in the mirror but said nothing. He cycled the glass panel that rose from its pocket to isolate the passengers in the back seat.

"Is your friend Tsosie following us?" David smiled easily and leaned back, reaxing.

"He left already and he'll meet us there," Rolan Begay said. "It's only a couple of miles. — Did you know, this is all checkerboard country."

As they drove, Begay explained, and David pretended to care. He had to humor the Indian if he hoped to get his help.

The land north of Gallup is checkerboard, Begay told him, 640-acre sections of originally Federal land, deeded to the railroads as incentive for laying track through the lightly populated west more than a century and a half ago. Those railroad sections, sold off long ago, alternate with sections held by the government and finally dedicated as Indian lands, segmented reservations. The difference today matters most to someone thirsty. On the reservation, no alcohol is available, at least officially. On privately owned lands there are bars, and clubs, and taverns, and, Rolan said, "what my father called drinking shops."

72

He was still explaining when he and David slipped into a booth at *The Wagon Wheel* where Buck Tsosie was waiting.

"He spent a lot of time in drinking shops, my dad did. Too much time," Rolan said. "I don't."

Tsosie was smearing a linked chain of damp circles on the tabletop with his sweating glass of iced tea. "Good story," he said. "But we're here now, and it's your party."

"No. It's his." Rolan nodded toward David, sitting across the table from them.

Tsosie said, "Where's your friend?"

"My driver," David said,

"Like a chauffeur, you mean?"

"Like a pain in the ass. They say Job had boils. I've got a 'driver.'" David waved a hand. "Let it go."

Rolan ordered a Coke from the barmaid.

"Vodka martini for me," David said. "Grey Goose."

Tsosie watched them both, watching the barmaid.

David took a breath and consulted his Rolex. "Okay," he said. "Let's do it. I'm here because I have a proposition for you, Rolan. You know as well as I do that a casino on the reservation is inevitable. The council has said as much. They've opened up the possibility for three or four of them, in fact. It'll come, next year, or the year after. It'll come, and I want to help you speed the day closer. Do you understand that?"

Rolan nodded.

David waited. "No opinion? No comment?"

Rolan turned to Tsosie. "Do I have an opinion?" he asked.

"Unless you've gone brain dead."

"Okay, what is it?"

"You're neutral right now, but you'd like more information. Like, why is Mr. David coming to you?"

Rolan and David both chuckled. David pointed at Tsosie and said, "Got it."

"Sometimes he's more direct," Rolan said.

"But he's usually right." Tsosie said nothing.

"I need help with the council," David said. "I've talked with Malcolm Obee, and he's in. He'll help as much as he can, and he thinks you could help too, if I make it worth your while."

"Did he say that?"

The barmaid interrupted with their drinks.

"Can I get you anything to eat? A menu? We got—"

"Take off!" David said.

The girl flinched but said nothing.

"Uh...sorry. — Look Honey. We'll call if we want you."

All three watched her hip-swiveled slouch back to the bar across the ill-lit room.

"It won't hurt to listen," Begay said.

David made his pitch — brief, direct, as enticing as he could make it. He offered Rolan the exclusive rights to gift shop and souvenir sales facilities in any casino managed by him—T. J. David—and the management team whose broad experience he planned to bring to the service of the Navajo people. "All I need from you in exchange is your support. Introduce me to the right council members. Persuade them to listen to my proposition. It's like pushing over a row of dominoes. One goes, the rest fall in line. Tell me who the first domino is." He waited. And watched.

"Ah, well," Rolan said. "There's a problem.

You might as well hear it right away. My sister won't be

real happy if I do that. You mention casinos to her, she starts foaming at the mouth."

"Does she know how much is involved? State-wide, the newspapers say, gaming in New Mexico's a three and a half billion dollar business a year. That's *billion,* with a Bee. One of the casinos down near Albuquerque is grossing sixteen million a month, just from slots. You think she could ignore a cash flow like that?"

Tsosie said, "Window Rock's a village. It's not Albuquerque."

"People will come," David said. "Vegas used to be a one outhouse truck stop...before my time."

He listed the advantages he and his associates offered. "It's a simple matter of business. Nothing complicated about it, for the right man. I've got six years experiences managing a major casino in Las Vegas. Friends and connections like you wouldn't believe. You'll need experienced catering people, and I've got them lined up. Everything to run a food operation, right down to the linen service and glassware for any cafe or restaurant in the casino. Vending machines sit in a corridor and generate more revenue than you'd ever guess. Untraceable income, if you own them...and service them yourself..

"Gaming equipment isn't cheap, even to lease, let alone buy. I've got connections who'll give me a twenty to thirty per cent discount from day one. I can have the slots and tables installed and running six weeks from the day I get the go ahead. Not the old mechanical crankers, either. Electronic slots! Even electronic blackjack tables, no dealers to pay...or supervise.

"Entertainment in the casino showroom... I know people

at the talent management agencies. It's the stars that make Vegas the world's number one tourist attraction. You want Celine Dion? Jerry Seinfeld? Brittany? Chinese acrobats? Strippers? Don Rickles? Whoever you want, I can get them. And there's more. A lot more.

"Let's do this. Let's get together tomorrow and let me lay it all out for you. I'll show you the numbers. In writing. If what I say makes sense, get me introductions to the right council members. That's all you have to do." David sat hunched over his martini glass, spinning it by the stem. His free hand tapped a tattoo on the tabletop. He forced himself to relax, watching Rolan Begay for a sign, some indication.

Begay said, "I've got to be back home tomorrow. In Albuquerque. I can't—"

"Not a problem. I'll come to Albuquerque. In a couple of days, wherever you say. ... How about it?"

Tsosie sat watching the pair, nothing in his expression revealed his opinion.

Rolan nodded slowly. "We can do that. Sure. Come see my shop, Begay's Indian Arts, in Old Town. You ought to know what kind of operation I run."

"Just give me the address."

The door opened and Artie Files strode in.

Rolan took out his business card and wrote a phone number on the back of it. "This is my cell. You can get me any time."

"David, you about done over here?" Files stood beside the booth. "I'm sitting outside there, twiddling my thumbs, wasting time, when I could be sweating up the sheets with that Sharon broad."

"Sharon Obee?" Rolan looked puzzled.

"She give me the come-on there in the restaurant. I'll go ring her chimes for her and—"

"Wait in the car!" David said. *Jesus!* That's all he needed, Files screwing up his play with some typical stupidity. "I told you to wait."

"You know how long I've been out there?"

Tsosie shook his head. "You think the way to Malcolm is through his wife?"

David rose and pointed toward the door. "Out, now!"

Files bristled but stumbled away, David close behind him. In the doorway David turned back to tell Rolan, "This is a misunderstanding," he said, pointing at Files. "I'll take care of it. And I'll see you at say noon, day after tomorrow." He pushed Files outside. The door slammed behind them.

Files whirled to poke David in the chest. "You lay a hand on me again, I'll break it off! The old man said baby-sit you, not take your shit!"

"Calm down, Files. When you get back to Vegas, you can report me to your hunky boss. Until then, you'll do what I tell you. To start with, you stay away from their women. And shut up when I'm trying to deal with these gomers. Now get in the car!"

Files jerked away, muttering curses.

David pretended not to hear.

Tsosie drained his glass of iced tea and waited for Rolan's comments. "Well?"

Rolan shrugged. "I can hear him out, see what he has to say. You know, he makes a kind of sense. The casinos *are* coming. Whether he can help the *Diné* handle all the problems that come along with them, I don't know."

"You know."

"How the hell do I know?"

"Don't get your shorts in a bunch, Rolan. You heard him. Help him and there's some 'profit' in it for you."

"He's probably right. He knows the way things work. He's trying to help."

"No, I said 'profit.' He's decided he can buy you. You think Leela's for sale?"

Rolan studied his empty Coke glass. "I didn't say I wanted anything from him."

"He told Malcolm not to worry about his share in all this. I was there, I heard him. Word for word, he said 'I'll take care of you. In a casino, with all that money moving through the place, there's a lot of leakage.' You like that term? *Leakage.*"

"You want to be there when we meet?"

"Uh-huh. I want to hear how this leakage thing works."

$ **13** $

Wince asked Elliott Chávez to meet him at the construction site at 7:00 a.m. Wince was there, parked on Lomas in his Mustang, at 6:30. Unable to sleep past 5:00 these mornings, he'd driven to the site early and parked at the curb, facing east.

It wasn't the same as having coffee in the North Valley and watching the shadow sweep define the Albuquerque morning. But this was another morning, and the sun rose here as well. He could turn his head and watch the New Mexico sunrise wash east to west down Route 66, lighting Four Hills in the east, the university area, and all the way down-slope west to downtown Albuquerque. His adoptive home the past ten years.

After bouncing from one Navy town to another as a kid while his dad alternated months of sea duty with tours spent at stations ashore—Norfolk, San Diego, Groton—Wince helped his parents move to Albuquerque, more than a day's drive from salt water. They opened *Dimmie's Half Off*, the restaurant that let Dimmie, retired now, use his Navy experience as a cook. Bob enrolled at UNM and had his future defined by the seduction of Southwestern Studies. Especially a pair of anthropology courses, and a single semester in architecture. That year and a half made a builder of him, in love with adobe and the squat homes that rise from the dun-colored earth anywhere from Mexico north past Santa Fe and Taos.

His indecision lasted two years longer, while he juggled part-time carpentry and classes that grew less and less interesting. The work turned fulltime when he dropped out of the university and joined Ernie Morales's construction crew. He could finish school later. He'd rather be a carpenter, for now, headed toward cabinet-making. And more.

He spent five years learning the business from Morales, endured a wasted year and a half in the joint for a crime he didn't commit, another year putting his life back together. But it was persuading Elliott Chávez to join him that turned things around. Chávez was someone who understood that work can be fun. Someone to bounce ideas off. Someone he trusted.

And taking on the complete remodeling of the abandoned Eastside Motel with Chávez was a test of the partnership. Sunrise Plaza was a great opportunity but also a major risk. That was why he couldn't sleep past 5:00 and woke every morning, eager to go to work and half-afraid not to.

He finished the coffee he'd picked up at Sonic and crushed the empty cardboard cup in one hand before cramming it back into the paper sack. It might be the first joke of the day. He owned a restaurant but bought coffee at someone else's drive-up window. Bad coffee at that, buck-thirty a cup. Hard to figure why.

Chávez was there at 6:55, appearing inside the temporary cyclone fence as if he'd spent the night locked in.. He took the padlock off the gate and walked into the street. He waved at

Wince and joined him in the Mustang when Wince popped open the passenger door and beckoned.

"You park out back in the alley?" Wince asked.

Chávez nodded. "Came in the back way," he said. "To leave the street free. If we get the whole crew parking out front here, neighbors will start bitching."

"Start?"

"So far we're still okay with everybody on the block, except the *viejo loco* on the corner. He walks his dogs by here every morning, giving us the fisheye. But he's the only one. No reason to have any more neighbors pissed off, this close to being finished. — Damn it!" Chávez pointed down the street. "Here comes Stapely. I told him noon, not till then." He pushed open the car door. "I'll take care of it."

Stapely parked his pickup at the curb but didn't turn off the engine. He rolled down his window.

Wince watched the two argue for no more than a minute. Stapely left a black smear of rubber on the pavement, screeching away.

Sandoval arrived next, then three others in a red Dodge Ram crew-cab with spinner hubs, and Mikey Bosco on his Ducati. By 7:05 the whole crew was there, only a couple of them carrying lunch pails or paper sacks. It was a morning half-day, for all but Stapely. A few wore low-slung loaded tool belts, like gunfighters striding Albuquerque's streets. Others arrived empty handed, their tools locked up in the ground floor retail unit B. Unit B had been designed to be the property manager's office. It was now a temporary foreman's plans shack, since Chávez had pulled the site trailer away to let the crew lay sod on the lot.

Wince walked through the unlocked gate to join the crew around the coffee urn he knew Chávez had fired up in the plans shack.

By 11:00 a.m. Wince had finished all the phone calls he was willing to make. For the third time, he stalled Ray Schwartz on the roofing bill he'd been staring at for several weeks. He promised to settle with the plumbing supply house by the end of the week...knowing he couldn't. And he called two of the buyers to remind them of the upcoming settlement, time and place. He described the completed work, a little stroking to keep the buyers committed. He closed his laptop, tucked his cell phone into a shirt pocket and looked up to see Tom Jones open the door.

Tom Jones—dusty boots, battered black Stetson—the man Chávez had described as "pure Texas bullshit, big hat, no horses."

Not a great morning.

"Janie Collier said you want to see me," Jones said.

"That's Janie for you. Always helping out."

"Was she wrong?"

"Coffee?" Wince flipped down the urn spigot and filled a styrofoam cup. He offered it to Jones.

"No cream left," he said. "But there's sugar." He pointed at the scatter of cups and sugar packets and Popsicle-stick stirrers spilled on the desktop beside the humming urn.

"Black's good." Jones took the cup and looked around.

"What do you need?"

"I just want to get caught up on what you're doing over at *Half-Off.*"

Nodding, Wince said, "Little remodeling, that's all."

"Did Dimmie tell you him and me had a good talk before he left?"

"If so, it was the first time."

"He must of told you."

"No, he didn't. So now you're going to." Wince leaned back and motioned for Jones to keep talking. Time to get this over with.

Nothing new in the proposal. The Hispanic Economic Caucus that employed Tom Jones as their lobbyist had decided on their next acquisition, *Dimmie's Half-Off*. "Their" restaurant would flourish under Hispanic ownership. "We're more'n half the population in Albuquerque, half your customers or more," Jones said. "We could—"

"Who's 'we?' You being Tom Jones now, or the famous Señor HO-nace?"

"You know what I mean! Us Hispanos. When you…." He took a deep breath. "Look, if Dimmie and me reached an understanding, you and me—"

"What understanding?" Wince saw Stapely trot past toward the rear of the site where the skeleton crew was finishing up in number four. "Lay it out for me."

"We talked about a group of us coming in on the restaurant. Investors, you know? Dimmie mentioned some improvements the restaurant needs."

"Funny. He didn't tell me."

"Then…what is it I see going on at *Half-Off*?

Looks like construction."

Wince nodded and let Jones make his pitch. Nothing new, the same unpersuasive arguments. But this time Jones was pumped, more intent. There was something personal in it. Something urgent. Wince didn't know what.

After a few grunts to show that he was listening and reward Jones for his vehemence, Wince craned to look out the window at the commotion in the courtyard but saw nothing. He heard the rasping scream of a power saw cycling on and off as someone pumped the trigger. Then the blurted punch of a nail gun.

"That's why I had to see you right away. My friends like the place the way it is. There's no sense changing anything yet. We got some ideas, and the money to pay for any redecorating. I know things are tight for you right now, and—"

"How do you know that?"

Jones looked around the room, pointing at scrap lumber piled in one corner, the strips of masking tape criss-crossing the display window, like tornado defense. "This motel thing has got you squeezed between rocks and a hard place, like they say. Everybody knows you're in too deep. Me and my friends could solve that. Think about it. No partnership on *Half Off*, nothing like that. I'm talking about an outright sale. You get the cash you need to finish work here. We get the restaurant." Jones paused, almost preening. "Dimmie would go for it. It s the best thing for you."

"Me?"

"Okay. For the both of us."

"Not for sale."

Shouting replaced the whine of the saw.

"Don't be so sure. When we—"

"Not for sale," Wince said. "Now or ever."

The shouting was louder now, two voices, really going at it.

Wince turned toward the commotion. "It's settled, Toe-
mas. Take off." He pushed through the back door into the
courtyard.

"You haven't heard our offer! Four hundred thousand,
cash!"

$ 14 $

Begay's Indian Arts was located at 1432 Los Arboles, only yards away from 1430, a private dwelling with eye-popping pink window frames like splashes of Pepto-Bismol on the tan stucco walls.

Files parked at the curb, under the broad-leaf umbrella of a huge cottonwood.

"Not here," David said. "Keep going. It's next door, the one with the sign."

Files turned off the ignition and faced David in the rear view mirror. "You can walk it. It's what, thirty feet? Right past the sign there, the one that says 'Loading Zone?' That means I don't park there. You walk."

David let it go. Files was a pain in the ass, but pushing him wouldn't do any good. David needed to be sharp, and cheerful, talking to Begay. He flipped open the manila folder on the seat beside him for a final check. "Okay. All set. You stay in the car," he said, and swung open the heavy limo door.

"Where'm I gonna go?" Files slouched behind the wheel and opened his crumpled copy of *Hustler*.

Begay was waiting at the counter in his shop. The place was bigger than it looked from the street. Subtle indirect lighting cast a warm glow over the glittering jewelry that filled the cases and counters and gave the room its definition. David spotted Tsosie behind a pair of hinged café doors separating the showroom from whatever storage or living quarters lay in the back. "Hello Rolan. ... And Tsosie."

Tsosie nodded.

"Come on in. Let me show you around," Begay said. "If you do open a casino on the rez, you're going to want a shop like this. Quality merchandise. Not plastic like some places." He smiled his pride and waved in an arc that took in his display.

David spent fifteen minutes taking the tour. He begrudged every minute of it. He was here to sell an idea, not to buy some Indian junk necklace, but he went along. Begay was enjoying it all…to David's advantage. David had learned a negotiating principle years ago. To win, get the other guy to say "yes" four times. About anything. Five or more times, you could sell him his own shoes. He led Begay into a series of agreements by seeming awed at the collection Begay flaunted for him.

"That's right," Begay said. "Unique. We keep the collection on display intact and sell replicas of each individual piece."

"And everything else here, the stuff in the other cases, is for sale?"

Begay nodded. "Everything."

Close enough to "yes." David had Begay hooked. But Tsosie hadn't said anything yet. He turned to involve him in what Begay didn't seem to understand was a negotiation. They followed Begay through the café doors.

The three sat at the small table in Begay's kitchen behind the shop and read through the prospectus David had prepared for them. They shared sour coffee and some kind of doughnutty Mexican things Begay called *sopaipillas*. Puffy and hollow, like filled doughnuts without the filling. Tsosie dribbled honey on his. David followed Begay's lead and ate his first lump of the dough dry. Dunking the next one didn't improve it.

At the end of thirty minutes, David had exhausted his arguments. Begay was still on the fence. And Tsosie hadn't even blinked.

David spread his budget papers on the table. "Do you see how much your tribe could profit from all this?"

"Yes, 'profit.' Good word for it." Tsosie didn't react to "tribe" and turned to Begay. "We ought to show Mr. David how a class operation like yours stands out from the rest."

David didn't know where this was headed. He braced to argue.

Begay shook his head. "I don't see what—"

Tsosie stood up, pushing his chair back. "Let me call Robert. He wants to show you the gift shop we're working on.

"Yes?"

"We'll go to *Half Off* for the comparison." He reached across the table to take Begay's cell phone and punch in a number. "Just wait."

David looked at Begay, who nodded. "Good idea," he said. "If Robert's there…"

The courtyard was empty. The shouting issued from number four where the door stood open. Wince passed two men screwing brass numerals to the doors of units one and three and ran across the courtyard to the open door. "What the hell's going on?"

Ordaz and Stapely stood shouting nose-to-nose, Stapely

in English, Ordaz in Spanish, neither listening to a word the other said. Stapely sputtered and spit in anger.

Ordaz jerked off his smeared glasses and waved them like a baton. *"¡Pendejo, yo me descuido un poco y tu haces tonterias!"*

"How long I have to wait for you? A fuckin' blind man could do your job. I can't—"

"Shut up, both of you!" Wince pushed between them and stiff-armed them apart. "Shut up, Stapely. And Luis, *itu cállate también!* Both of you. Shut up and tell me what the hell this is."

Their explanations overrode each other. Stapely had wasted three days waiting for Ordaz to finish a simple job. Ordaz had been frustrated by this incompetent *gringo* carpenter hanging over his shoulder. They shouted the same gripes and proved nothing but mutual antipathy. Then, volume decreasing, tempo slowing, the two men relaxed knotted fists and looked away from Wince. Finally, backing down.

Wince let them sputter and fume and said nothing. He waited for one of them, then both, to resign and look to him for a solution. A nail gun lay on the floor. He kicked it away. An electric saw sat atop scraps of firring strips and one-by-fours near the baseboard. Drywall dust frosted everything. He picked up a 40-penny spike from the floor. It was five inches long and didn't belong here. He tossed it in the air, flipping it. Twice. Then he pointed at the new wall patch. "Open that up," he said.

Stapely exploded. He spun a half circle and threw up his hands. "What the fuck! This is what I knew—"

"Open the damn wall! Now!" Wince reached for Stapely but stopped short of touching him.

He did touch Ordaz, laying a hand on his chest to push him gently toward the corner. *"Cálmate Luis. ¡Todo está bien!"* Wince stepped out the door and pointed across the courtyard. "Danny, Joe, go get Elliott and bring him in. He's out with the paving guys." He ducked back into apartment number four.

In three minutes, Wince watched Chávez and two of his crew come in from the parking lot out back where they were laying pre-cast cement curbstones. "Bring them in," he told Chávez, and pushed his way between Sandoval and a tiler everybody called "Wheezer," standing in the doorway.

"*¿Qué pasó?*" Chávez said.

Wince pointed at the far wall, gaping open below the chair rail molding to reveal the vent- and soil-pipes for the bath beyond and the kitchen sink drains. "Small problem," he said. "Take a look." He held Chávez's arm and turned him to see a display.

Clay Stapely was nailed to the wall.

Not standing there. Not leaning against it.

Nailed to the wall.

Wince talked to the men clustered in the doorway. "Stapely just made screw-up of the week. Y'see him?"

They nodded. They saw him. Wheezer whistled under his breath.

"Now take off. Everybody. Finish your job and punch out."

Chávez walked over to examine Stapely, who stood fuming but said nothing. A fistful of denim from each pants leg and both shirt cuffs were nailed to the wall. The nailgun lay on the floor. Kneeling at the opened wall, Luis Ordaz pried loose a pair of 40-penny spikes that were punched through the PVC soil-pipe a foot above the floor.

Wince motioned out the door. Chávez left for the court-yard.

"Hey!" Stapely said. "What the fuck! You can't leave me..."

He shut up when he saw the look Wince turned his way.

Wince joined Chávez outside.

Chávez said, "What's it about?"

"I guess Ordaz was slow swapping out the ceramic pipe with PVC, so Stapely got pissed off and spiked the soil pipe."

"He what? What's that mean, *espiked* it?"

"Those forty-penny spikes form a cross, like a grid, inside the pipe. In a week or two, accumulation would plug up the pipe, and we'd be cursing Ordaz's lousy work while we rip out the wall to get at it," Wince said. "By then, Stapely would be long gone, and maybe we'd blame Ordaz."

Chávez started back into the apartment.

Wince grabbed his arm. "Let it go, Elliott. It's done."

"But...who nailed Stapely...?" He found the answer in Wince's smile. "You did it, *verdad*?"

"I thought he ought to stand there until Ordaz finishes. Just to see the work."

"And then?" Chávez watched three of their men across the courtyard. The three lounged against the far wall and feigned disinterest, counting birds in the empty sky.

"Then Stapely can seal the wall again, and we can get the damn place ready to sell! Okay?"

"What do we do with Stapely?"

"I want to kick the crap out of him, but I think we're better off leaving him where he is for an hour. The embarrassment's worse for him than a beating. ... I know. Have you got your Polaroid in the car?" At Chávez's nod, Wince said. "Get it. I want to give him a reminder of all this."

"Okay."

"Then take him down," Wince said. "Have him frame and drywall the hole, pay him off and fire his ass."

Chávez nodded. "How did you know that thing about *espiking* the soil pipe?"

"I saw it when we cleared a plugged drain-line at Manzano High three, four years ago, when I was still working for Morales. Today Ordaz and Stapely were chipping at each other. I walked in on them and found a forty-penny spike Stapely dropped on the floor, but the gun he's using takes two-and-a-half inchers."

"Stapely's a devious sucker." Chávez said. "Like you."

"Takes one to know one."

Chávez nodded. "I heard that. Thanks, let me check on Stapely."

"You want to turn him loose?"

"Sweat him awhile."

Wince slapped Chávez's raised hand and called to the waiting crew members. "It's over! Finish up what you were doing and take off."

Wince went into number four to discuss Stapely's future with him.

$ **15** $

A black stretch Lincoln with Nevada commercial plates was parked outside *Dimmie's Half Off* when Wince got there, summoned. The driver sat at the wheel, seat tilted back, eyes closed, mouth agape, sound asleep. Inside the restaurant, Rolan and Buck waited with a third man wearing a nubby silk suit.

"Sorry," Wince said. "I had to pick up something." He carried a package wrapped in brown butcher paper. He ripped it open to reveal an ornate certificate. "I had to get this framed.

Rolan said, "Say hello to Tee Jay David. He's here to see what you and Buck are up to. ...Tee Jay, meet Bob Wince, the friend I told you about before."

The two shook hands, after Wince tucked the framed certificate under his arm.

"Mr. Wince," David said. "Good to meet you...in person. Not on the phone."

"My pleasure. ...Buck, take this, okay? Your license." He held it up on display, then handed it over. ***B.I.A. Approved Site***, it read, above two lines of smaller type. "Hang it where people can see it. Maybe behind the register there." *Another piece for the crazy quilt,* Wince thought.

Buck Tsosie took the certificate. "I'll find a place for it. Thanks, Robert."

Rolan said, "Tee Jay has been talking to the *Diné* Council about him managing a casino on the rez. You know, manage it for us. If it works out, I might be running the casino gift shop for him, I don't know. In the meantime..." He turned to Tsosie "I asked him to come see what we're doing here," Tsosie said. "You want to give him the tour?"

"The place is yours, then?" David said to Wince.

"Half mine. Actually forty-nine percent. Buck's the boss, with the other fifty-one."

"*You* are?" David asked Tsosie.

"I was as surprised as you," Tsosie said. "When Robert decided to put in a gift shop, he made me a partner."

"*Majority* partner?"

"We signed the papers a while ago."

"Pretty generous." David examined Wince.

"It's a *gift* shop, right?" Tsosie couldn't restrain a smile. "It was Christmas time, that's all I could figure. Maybe it was a Christmas gift. You know, *Diné* and the pueblo peoples, most of us, when we elect the council, new council members share their good fortune. They give out gifts at their installation. So here we are. Robert's expanding. His business is taking off like gangbusters, lots of good fortune, and he decides to share it with the unworthy. Like me. Maybe that's it."

Wince said, "Buck's modest. He's smarter than I am, a better salesman. I'm too busy to run a store, even if I knew how. Anyway, the gift shop should be Native American, like Rolan's place. That creates a few advantages." He pointed at the framed certificate Tsosie still held.

"So this is technically your place," David said to Tsosie. "And you're Navajo?"

"*Adopted* Navajo," Tsosie said. "I think my people came up from *Tlaxcala.*"

David looked puzzled.

"A small state in Mexico, maybe the smallest," Wince said.

"There you are. Small, obscure, unimportant, like…I don't know like what. Like me," Tsosie said. "Navajos are important, 'cause Hollywood says so. Notice, you never see a movie Indian isn't Navajo, the noble ones, or maybe a killer Apache, or Sioux. But *Tlaxcalan's?* Whoever heard of them." Buck said, "So I can claim to be *adopted* Navajo, anyway. That means—"

Wince interrupted. "We're working on that," he said. "Right now, let me show you around Buck Tsosie's gift shop… used to be a restaurant." He snatched a Dasani bottle off the counter and handed it to Tsosie. "You want to take this out to Mr. David's driver? See if he wants some coffee."

"Skip it," David said. "He doesn't need anything."

"It's okay," Tsosie said to Wince, leaving. "You show him around." He laid the certificate on the counter.

"There's not much to see," Wince said. "This was the restaurant part, or maybe call it a 'coffee shop.' Not a dining room. More like a counter for burgers and fries. … The kitchen's back here." He stepped over the pair of slot machines on the floor and led the way. "Watch your step there."

David looked at the slots, then scanned the room as if looking for others. "Bayer 310s," he said. "They must be twenty years old! Do they still work?"

"Well enough for us," Wince said. "Back this way."

Wince pointed out the kitchen facilities. Freezer and cooler. Storage space, more crucial to a restaurant's success than diners recognize. Garbage disposal and dishwasher and more storage and cabinets, a grill and range and ovens and chemical fire-suppressing exhaust hood and prep tables and pastry proofer and oven and more storage cupboards and shelves. None of it seemed to impress or even interest David.

The banquet hall did. Wince watched David measure the space with a glance, then pace off the room's dimensions while feigning idle wandering. More than triple the size of the kitchen and dining room combined, it was a cavernous, echoing space, used now for little except yet more storage— soft goods and disposables, odd pieces of furniture, backup soft drink dispenser, even a Wurlitzer knock-off juke box.

"No coffee," Tsosie said, rejoining them. "He took the water."

"What's that thing?" David said. He pointed at a mounted animal head on the far wall. It looked like a jackrabbit with antelope pronghorns.

"Buck? You tell him," Wince said.

Tsosie bounced forward, as if on cue. "The jacklope is a rare hybrid creature," he said, lecturing. "You know, in England they call a bunny rabbit a 'coney,' like the Coney Island back east. And what we call a jackrabbit—that's a rabbit with jackass ears—the English call a hare. Hares and coneys and rabbits, all like different hybrids. Or half-breeds. And here in New Mexico we're mostly half-breeds. Me for instance. And Robert. And that jackalope…it's half jackrabbit, they say, and half antelope."

"Like pluots," Wince said.

The others looked at him, bewildered.

"It's a new fruit, half plum, half apricot."

"If you say so." David dismissed the example with a wave

of his hand and looked from Tsosie to Wince. "How big is this room?" he asked.

"I don't know."

"You don't know?"

"Roughly eighty on a side. Load-bearing perimeter walls, I-beamed roof, no partitions."

David shook his head. "If it was mine, I'd know how big it is."

"It used to be a warehouse." Wince said.

"So what? That's no—"

"It's bigger than I need, that's all. Might as well be a roller rink."

"Is it insulated?"

"Yeah, it's got a new fifteen thousand BTU heat pump, with wiring for a second unit. R-20 insulation in the walls. We're on city gas. But the room's so big, my dad never used it much. Maybe a couple times for wedding receptions, big parties like that."

"The parking lot outside, that's yours too?"

"The truck stop next door shut down. My dad bought the lot. Four acres. I don't know what he was going to do with it. We never had enough business here to need five hundred parking spaces."

"Really? Five hundred? How do you know that?"

"You measure the site and do the math. Four acres, at forty-three thousand, five hundred sixty square feet per acre. You leave twenty-five foot lanes between parking ranks, eight-and-a-half feet per car average. It works out to four hundred ninety seven cars." Wince watched David following along, doing the math in his head.

"You sure of that?"

Wince was sure, but he shrugged. Let David doubt him, if it pleased him. "It's all in the numbers."

"You ever park five hundred cars out there?"

"Not a chance!" Wince laughed. "On a big day my dad got maybe fifteen or twenty cars at once. So the lot's not striped for five hundred. But it could be."

"Uh-huh, fine." David stopped asking questions and spent his time peering into corners and nodding. He looked, said nothing, and walked. And nodded. For three minutes.

And chewed his lip.

Back in the restaurant, Wince said, "That's the whole thing. But mainly we're interested in finishing up the gift shop."

"You have plans you could show me? Architect's drawings?"

"We don' need no estinkin' drawin'ss," Buck Tsosie said, squinting at them.

Wince smiled.

David didn't.

"Robert's a builder, and designer," Tsosie said. "He can do the work himself."

"Uh-huh, fine." David stopped listening.

"As soon as we finish the other job," Wince said.

When David didn't ask about 'the other job,' Wince turned to Rolan Begay. "Does that do it?"

"That's the whole tour."

"Buck and I thought Tee Jay would like to see it. He saw the turquoise and our display cases, but what you're doing here is different."

"Looks like a truck stop," David said. "Or it might, if you

get it finished. Rolan's shop is more what I have in mind."

Wince walked them back through the kitchen to the front door. He offered them a cup of coffee but—passing the waitress service area—was glad that no one accepted the offer. Janie had finished cleaning the back counter. The place smelled like Comet. Both Pyrex coffee servers were empty, a pair of gleaming globes tipped upside down beside the electric burners.

"Thank you, Mr. Wince," David said. "All very interesting. ...Rolan? I'll come by tomorrow. We need to work out your approach to the council.... And Buck? You think you could join us?"

Tsosie shrugged. "If it's not too early. I need my sleep, you know? Six hours sleep, you're fine all day. Less than that, you can't even digest your food. I read this piece about—"

"Good, fine, we'll discuss your diet tomorrow. —Is that a *Tlaxcalan* thing?" David asked Wince, shaking his head.

Wince knew the feeling. Except, he enjoyed Buck's stories.

"Tomorrow," David said, as he left, hurrying as if to avoid any more conversation.

Files sat slumped behind the wheel, open magazine and empty Dasani bottle in his lap. David had to rap a tattoo on the driver's window with a quarter before Files bolted upright, shaking off sleep.

"Unlock!" David said. He climbed into the back seat, careful not to seem hurried. He looked straight ahead, ignoring Wince in the restaurant doorway behind him and the two Indians walking to Tsosie's truck. He whispered to Files, "Get moving! Let's go."

"I'm going." He tossed the empty Dasani bottle out the window and turned the ignition key. They pulled out of the paved parking lot and onto the frontage road beside I-25.

David watched Tsosie's pickup turn south, toward the intersection with I-40, heading away from them. He waited a moment, then relaxed. "There's a Hilton a mile ahead. I'll be staying there. You take the car back to Vegas and tell—"

"What? What's that mean, 'take the car back'? You know how far that is? It's like a fuckin' ten-hours trip! I'm not driving—"

"Tell Mr. Tedesco I'll call him."

Files looked back over his shoulder. "Mr. Tedesco said I should stay with you."

"I say you shouldn't."

"Well I'm damn sure not driving back there. What's the matter with you? I can turn the car in at the airport rental place and fly home. You ever think of that?"

"Okay, you do that. Then you can fly back home and tell Mr. Tedesco—"

"I can phone him, for God's sake! And you don't *tell* Mr. Tedesco nothing. He gets pissed."

"No, he'll be happy. Tell him I'll call, and he'll like what I have to say. —Here! This exit. Drop me at the Hilton." David leaned back against the soft leather seat. Today the car felt roomy and comfortable.

He drummed on both knees with his fingertips. The idea was coming. He'd seen the rainbow and could picture the pot of gold.

$ **16** $

Friday night, Wince was balancing his accounts for the third time in a week, looking for mistakes, or oversights, or uncommitted assets. A few dollars more. At 7:00 p.m. the phone interrupted, when Leela called. She was just home from school and wanted to change their weekend plans. She told him she'd drive down in the morning, get there before noon, and asked him to meet her at Tingley Beach.

"No, it's my turn to drive," Wince said. "It's no problem."

"Tingley Beach, about eleven-thirty, okay?" She hung up.

So here he sat, parked at Tingley, Saturday morning, watching the bulging muddy expanse of the Rio Grande sliding south. Hundreds of miles north, the Colorado snowpack was melting, filling the Rio Grande, sending drinking water and irrigation south through New Mexico into Texas. And three fishermen stood on the riverbank, fishing for trout, they told him when he asked. They'd he happy to snag some carp.

In the back seat of his Mustang, Wince had a picnic waiting. Cokes and sandwiches from *Subway*, folding chairs and table from the storage room at *Half Off.* He didn't know why Leela had decided to take the three-hour drive. She didn't enjoy the highway any more than he did. Something was up.

He tilted the driver's seat back and closed his eyes. Something he'd said. Or done. Something had him crosswise with

Leela. She needed more attention, and it was exhausting…if worth it.

They never quarreled. They'd hit it off from their very first date, lunch at the hot new yuppie place in Old Town, *Tierra Linda*. First "date," but their fifth meeting. Two conversations at Rolan's gift shop, another at a greasy spoon in Grants and the fourth at her double-wide outside Gallup, none of them a "date." Rolan had been with them every one of those times. *Between* them, Wince thought. Until that day at *Tierra Linda*….

Outside *Tierra Linda*, he parked his Mustang at the curb. Leela was smiling, sitting close beside him. Wince held out his hand and took a risk. "The worst embarrassment is the first time you go to kiss someone," he said. "You ask yourself 'Should I? Does she want me to?' It's tough, and I want to get past it. I mean, we both know it's coming, right?"

She didn't answer.

He pulled her closer, braced to feel resistance. It wasn't there.

He kissed her.

"Nice," she said. "Thank you."

"My pleasure." Silly conversation. Like they were 16 again.

"Mine too." She smiled at him. "Let's eat."

The tables and chairs at *Tierra Linda* were shining golden waxed pine. Tented napkins in a dozen colors brightened the tabletops. Fanned beside them were spoons, knives and forks with colored ceramic handles. Anorexic smiling waiters and waitresses wore jeans and starched white shirts, unbuttoned two-down on the boys, three- or four-down on the girls,

Every dish on the menu suffered California blight—mandarin oranges or kiwi in the pasta, almonds in the soups, the bitter fungus of arugula garnish spreading everywhere.

After Leela blinked at the first taste of her salad, Wince said, "We should have gone somewhere else."

"No, I'm flattered you picked this place. You go to some restaurants to eat. Others, you pick for a date. I think we're on a date."

Wince nodded.

"Is this the kind of place you'd pick out go if you weren't trying to impress me?"

"Probably not." He felt as if she'd caught him at something.

Their conversation turned out to be less fencing than Wince expected. It was easy and comfortable. Sharing likes and dislikes, starting with food. As they ate, they measured each other, offered vague histories, drifted from one topic to another, and got around to describing the type of restaurants they enjoyed.

"Hash houses for me," she said. "Not the white-tablecloth yuppie spots Rolan likes."

"Would you bring Rolan here?"

"Oh, he's probably been here. He's headed for 'respectable,' so he's always perfecting his tastes."

"He's respectable enough," Wince said.

"For you. And me. Not for some of the Elders. Rolan and I carry Anglo genes from an Irish grandfather."

"Is that a problem?" He motioned for the waitress to top up Leela's iced tea.

"Really, a great-grandfather, named Clancy, believe it or not—a railroad worker who came through Gallup laying track and teenage girls. He got three or four pregnant, married two of them, then took off. He left little Clancys all over McKinley County. Great-grandpa Clancy was one of them."

"Yeah, there's something Irish about you," Wince said.

"So to some of the Elders, Rolan and I aren't really *Diné*. But most accept us as if we were." She waved away their server and her pitcher of tea. "How about you? Do you know the word *coyote*?" She pronounced it *coy-OH-teh*.

"Sure. Mixed blood. Maybe half-Hispanic, half-Anglo."

"Politically correct for 'half-breed,' or maybe 'less-than-pure.' Like Rolan and me. They say *coyote* to your face, *cholo* behind your back. And you too…half-respectable."

"Me?" Then he smiled. "Which is my respectable half, Wince, or Filipino?"

"Okay, you're on your way up. Maybe you'll get over. Work hard, have the biggest construction company in New Mexico, a new house with your own stables on the golf course at *Las Campanas*. And so what? You'll still be coyote."

"You know about pluots?"

"What's a pluot?"

"They came from California, I think. Half plum, half apricot. They're really good. Juicy."

"Apricot lovers would still call them 'half-breed,' if that's your point."

"One thing about New Mexico," he said. "That stuff doesn't matter here."

"It matters less, maybe, but it matters. A guy as bright as you are, why doesn't that bother you?"

'Bright,' she'd said. He'd often been called casual, *laid back*, accused of being 'unconcerned.' That was probably meant as an insult, from that redhead, Phyllis Something, the night she dumped him. But 'bright' was a new one.

"You think?" Not quite fishing.

"I saw what you did for Rolan's store. I see how you feel about your work."

His 'work' wasn't work, if he could do it his way. He'd be happy building one house at a time. Adobe, hand-finished, comfortable. He could be happy at it, but 'happiness' wouldn't feed him.

"Did you ever watch a man build his own *hogan*?"

"Wow! Where' did that come from?" Wince took the bill from their waitress.

"You pick out a wife...or maybe she picks you. You build your *hogan* for the two of you. Oh, your family may help some, but there's no contractor you can hire to build your home. No contractor would have the same attitude you'd have."

"Maybe not."

"Buck does, I think. He's ready to build his own *hogan*. You might like to watch him do it."

Wince nodded. He knew he would. Surprising him, she knew it too.

"Pine and piñon frame, thatching, willow-wand walls daubed with mud." She stared into spaced, trying to recall details.

Wince signed the credit card slip and without effort recited the lines that came to mind. "I will arise and go now, and go to Innisfree, and a small cabin build there, of clay and wattles made."

"God! You are something!" Leela said. She cocked her head. "You think Yeats was secretly *Diné*? Building his own *hogan*?"

Wince's grin was so wide it hurt.

"How do you know Yeats?" she asked.

"Even dropouts remember some things they read."

"If Rolan remembered any poetry, he wouldn't admit it." She took his hand and pulled him toward the door. "Let's get to your car," she said. "I've got to kiss you again."

That was the meal he remembered best.

Today's picnic threatened to be different. He tried to anticipate and started compiling a mental list of his failings. The list was slow in coming. Sleep overtook him.

He woke at Leela's rapping on his window, jerked awake, blinking in the bright sunshine, and wiped his chin.

"Sorry I'm late," she said, when he fumbled to open the window. "An accident and traffic snarl near Sky City held me up. A tour bus and a van full of hunters crosswise in the road. Nobody hurt, but it was a real mess. ... Are you okay?"

"I'm bushed," Wince said.

"That's why I'm here. Because you're always bushed." She leaned through the open window and kissed him on the cheek "Are you awake?"

"I'm getting there," he said. "Do that again."

She motioned him out of the car. "Let's walk over to the river. I brought you a picnic." She lifted a basket on display, then cocked her head. "Okay?"

"Good idea." Wince glanced at his own surprise, waiting in the Mustang's back seat, but said nothing. He took the basket from Leela to carry it and followed her to a bench near the river.

It took two sandwiches, a Bud Light, and fifteen awkward minutes before Wince decided to risk a question. When no subtle approach occurred to him, he took a breath and blurted out, "What's going on?" He braced for the answer. "Why the conference?"

"You don't know?"

"I think there's something bugging you, and I probably did it. I don't know what, but... We might as well get right to it. I've got so much going down right now that I—"

"*That's* the problem, everything you're juggling. Robert, it's too much!"

"I planned to drive up today. Busy or not, you know I was—"

"There!" she said. "Coming to see me, it's hours, almost a full day you could spend on something else."

"Okay, sure, I've got things to do, but—"

"It's a long list."

"I guess. But—"

"I don't have to be first on your must-do list, but I have to be on it somewhere."

"You know you—"

"I don't know anything!" Leela bounced to her feet and walked away. She whirled back to face him. "Let me give you the whole list. Your dad dumped *Half Off* on you, and took off, that fast." She snapped her fingers.

"He found a perfect retirement job," Wince said, "on the base at Coronado, managing the PX lunch counter. He's got friends there, old navy buddies. He—"

"That does nothing for you. The restaurant he stuck you with, that's going to take sixteen hours a day. You and Elliott spend ten hours a day on the motel. What's that come to? Twenty-six?"

"No, we're okay. We—"

"You're worried about money all the time."

"Leela, I—"

"Let me finish!" She walked toward him, threatening to step on his toes, backing him toward the bench. "First, you've got some new project going with Buck, besides the gift shop, something about tracing his family, that's what he says. That's a couple of hours more each day. Two, the cops keep looking at you for I-don't-know-what."

"Cops? What do you mean?"

"That detective, Chutters. He asked what you're doing these days. Follow up on the turquoise theft, he said."

"That's his job, being curious."

"What *are* you doing?"

Wince considered telling her about the ruined adobe house he'd found at Elephant Butte, his next project. She might understand his wanting to get away from the pressure and spend some time working on his own house. But not now. The wrong time. He smiled to divert her while he thought of a way to tell her what he was doing. The smile didn't work.

"Forget Chutters. To top it all, now I find out..." She

turned away, folding her arms…"you're helping those slugs from Las Vegas!"

"You mean David, the Vegas guy? You think I'm—"

"You know how I feel about that."

"Rolan and Buck asked me to show them around *Half-Off*, and I gave them the nickel tour. Ten minutes, it was over. They never even mentioned a casino. Or Window Rock."

"Did you think I wouldn't find out you're getting involved?"

"There's nothing to find out!"

"Buck says you're playing him. Slick David. Like that's supposed to reassure me." She stared at him, obviously waiting for something more. "Well?"

He shook his head. "So it's all the casino thing, that's got you upset?"

"Not 'upset,' Robert. Upset's way too genteel. I'm *pissed!* And the casino is a time bomb. It could wreck everything!"

He took her hand, led her to the bench, and sat down beside her. "I promise," he said. "Maybe it's more solution than problem."

"Solution to what? What are you doing?"

He tucked her hand under his arm. One of the three fishermen walked past them. He'd given up. There were only two of them at the river now. "Nothing to worry about," Wince said. "Look. In a couple of weeks, everything will clear up."

"You mean that? Two weeks?"

"Two weeks. … Or maybe three."

She jerked away. "There! You're off again!"

"I'll admit I've been busy. But not for much longer. It won't take—"

"It better not." she said. Still angry, but calmer and less agitated.

"So let's eat," he said. "I've got nothing else to do...for an hour, anyway." He mugged for her, get her to laugh off her mood. "Then Elliott and I have to—"

"Robert!" She swatted him on the arm and shook her head. But she did smile.

$ **17** $

Artie Files stood in Mr. Tedescu's outer office and flexed and tried to bulk up, for Sheree. He posed with his hands clasped at his waist, pulled with the left, resisted with the right. Then he reversed the process. It was a neat trick. One set of muscles put a load on another, like weight-lifting without having to lug around a set of free weights.

"Are you okay?" Sheree said.

"Better than okay, lotta chicks'll tell you." Files clenched his buttocks and tilted his pelvis upward, pinching his belt. Almost like a standing crunch. He held it and pumped, internally, good for the lower abs. And it showed off his package. For Sheree. He could see the hunger in her eyes. Like that fuckin' squaw who come onto him over at Window Rock, then changed her mind and tried backing out.

"You want to have a seat?"

"No thanks, Honey. Gotta do eight more reps." He recognized her curiosity. Like admiration. "If you wanna know, it's a real old system. I read it on the back of this comic book I found once. A guy named Charles the Atlas invented it. 'Dynamic Tension,' they call it. Works real good."

He rotated his head to the left and pulled his neck down into the collar of his polo shirt. It corded up his neck, gave him a real strong look.

Sheree half-rose from her desk and said, "Please, Mr. Files. Please set down tilll Mr. Tedescu can see you."

"How long's that gonna be?"

"Oh good! Now!" she said, pointing at the red light flashing above the double doors in the far wall. "Now. Just go in. He'll see you now."

"And I'll see you later," Files said, winking at her. "We can get together, like tonight, what do you think?" He had this one going, he could tell. Couple drinks, a cinch, even without the rufy.

The girl went back to reading her magazine.

Files knew she was trying to play cool. He puckered up and blew a kiss on the way past her desk.

Inside the throne room, Files waited for Mr. Tedescu to speak first. Mr. Tedescu was perched on his big chair like some high muckety-muck, making like he was so busy that little people had to wait to talk to him till he was ready. Which was always later. Files teetered from heel to toe, pressing the arch of each foot hard against the floor, counting. Twenty-two reps till Mr. Tedescu looked at him.

"Where is Tee Jay David?" Mr. Tedescu tugged his tie tighter and shot his cuffs, preparing for this interview. He was dressed in mossy green today. Really weird. "You were instructed to stay with him."

"He sent me back," Files said.

"I sent you with him. When two instructions come into conflict, which one do you heed?"

"Uh…what?"

"If I give you an order, I expect you to obey that order."

"I will! I will, Mr. Tedescu. Just say what you want me to do."

"I want you to stay with Tee Jay, right beside him, whatever the circumstance. But you can't do that now, can you? He's not here."

"I don't think nobody's after him, if you're worried. The ones you said wanted to cap him, I ain't seen a one."

"That's not all you haven't seen. But I'm not really interested in your inattention, you understand that?"

"Uh…probly."

"I need to know his activities, Artie my friend. Not your understanding of his activities, you…" His voice faded away.

That warned Files. The old man was pissed, pretty clear, because he was turning quiet. When he spoke soft, that meant trouble. When he whispered, Artie knew to seek cover. "I could go back, if you say so. Only David said to tell you, it's all gonna work out. You'll be happy, he said. He thinks he solved the problem."

"Solved what?"

"The problem you and him had."

Mr. Tedescu said, "What solution?"

"Oh, he never said. But I figured it out. He's got a couple of those Indian bozos working for him up there on the reservation. like his 'assistants.'" He drew quotation marks in the air with his forefingers. "These assistants, they're connected. They'll work it that he gets to run the new casino they're gonna maybe build. I think."

"Tee Jay trusts these Indians?"

"What's it matter? They'll do what he wants. They're okay. And good looking, some of them. It'd surprise you. You ought to see this one squaw I met there. Young one, a great rack, you know, and—"

Mr. Tedescu shook his head. "Tee Jay's smarter than they are, isn't he? Certainly more clever."

There it was. One of Mr. Tedescu's confusing questions. Sometimes he wanted an answer. Sometimes he asked a question nobody could answer, like thinking out loud. And Files had to decide which this was. "Smarter than what, Mr. Tedescu?"

"The survey team I sent in there six months ago got *bupkis* from the Indians. Does David believe he can do better?"

"Well...he's real smart." Files watched for the old man's reaction.

"I think so too."

Files nodded. Okay! He'd got that one right! "Yeah, David's real smart," he said. "So...okay if I go?"

Mr. Tedescu stood.

Files flinched. What the hell was this? He'd never seen Mr. Tedescu on his feet before. "I'm sorry!" he said. It was all that came to him. And he flinched again when Mr. Tedescu spoke softly, almost a whisper.

"Go back to Albuquerque. Stay there until Tee Jay is ready to come home. From now on you call me every morning. On this line." He scribbled on a business card and flipped the card to Files. "Call me at seven every morning. I—"

"*Seven* o'clock?"

Mr. Tedescu stared him down. "Make it six." He sat on his throne again. "Six a.m., every morning, and you'll report on where Tee Jay is staying, who he met with, what he accomplished the day before. If you know."

Files digested his orders. He said. "But if I don't know...?"

"You will phone me every day at six a.m., until I require otherwise." He sat down in his big chair.

Files nodded, and blinked, and waited for the rest.

"Leave."

"Yes sir.... You mean... leave? Now?"

Mr. Tedescu had folded his hands and was looking at something on the ceiling. Files couldn't see what.

Then to top it all, Sheree wasn't at her desk when Files walked out. Helluva note.

$ 18 $

"**What's holding things** up?" Eloy Sanchez said. "We have the money. You've got the contact, you've been telling me."

Tom Jones chewed his pencil stub for a moment, then spat out the bitter shreds. He examined the stub before he dropped it in the ashtray. It was a yellow Dixon Ticonderoga, #2, but the brand didn't matter. One pencil tasted pretty much like another. "We can still make it work," he said. The little short golf pencils were the best. Like chewing a fat toothpick. And no erasers to crumble in your mouth. No rubber crumbs between your teeth.

One of the Sanchez twins asked, "How do we do it?"

Jones didn't know which one she was, Agnes or Doris. They were both short and pretty. They both talked too much. It was their father whose opinion mattered. The four of them sat around a table in Eloy Sanchez's kitchen, Jones and Sanchez planning, the girls doing the girl thing. Interrupting.

"I may have to do some negotiating with Wince," Jones said. "Will the board authorize me to dicker with him, or do you want to set a price limit first?"

"What do you think?"

Jones took a red golf pencil from his jacket pocket and bit down. It didn't taste red. "Wince is stubborn, but I'm pretty sure I can bring him around."

"First you said we could get the restaurant for next to

116

nothing. Now you say Wince isn't selling."

"When he paid off Dimmie's mortgage, that wiped out our leverage. I don't know where the money came from. But maybe we've got another chance, 'cause Wince needs money again. He's up to his ass in debt. Excuse me, girls."

Both girls tittered. "Up to his ass," Agnes or Doris said.

"Who's he owe?" Eloy Sanchez looked at the splintered pencil stub in the ashtray and brushed nothing off his lip. He waited for an answer.

"The bank." Jones said. "He took out a construction loan, and—"

"I'll take it over. You know, buy the loan."

"You mean like, make him refinance with you?" Jones sought patience. He took a breath and admired the granite counter tops here in the Sanchez kitchen. He added more sugar to his coffee. He smiled at the girls. Finally he said, "The bank wouldn't sell you his loan."

"Why not? I've bought fifty car loans from a bank, six or seven home mortgages. It's a simple process. Clear any liens, execute quit-claims, make certain that he doesn't owe anyone else. When I buy up his debts, he has to come looking for help. I know people who—"

"Why'nt you can talk to Wince, Daddy?"

"Or we could talk to him for you, Agnes and me. He's like, kind of cute, you know?" She winked at her sister. Agnes, the other one, on his left. The one with the squint.

"No!" Jones stood, scraping his chair over the tile floor, and went to refill his coffee cup from the carafe on the counter. That's all he needed. Lose his chance... "I can take care of it," he said.

"There are other properties," Sanchez said.

"C'mon, Eloy!" Jones could feel everything slipping away. "You know what they say. Location, location, location. There's no other places that near 'the Big I.' You know, where the two interstates meet." And none, Jones didn't say aloud, whose acquisition would make him a full partner in the project, and prove himself to the Caucus. Earn his way into a leadership position. He was just as much Hispanic as the rest of them. Just as much as *pinche* Eloy Sanchez with his blonde mother. But cursed by his Anglo name, Jones needed to prove himself. He needed a success. *Half-Off* was it.

"Is it really economics?" Sanchez asked. "Or is this pride? You want *Half Off* because Dimmie turned you down. Now his boy kicks your ass, too. Excuse me, girls."

They giggled. "Kicks your ass."

"Trust me on this, Eloy. I know how to handle Wince."

"We'll see. ... What'll the place go for?"

"With the big new parking lot, I estimate four-seventy. Without it, say he wants to split the lot off, maybe three-fifty."

"*You* estimate?"

"Okay, I'll get Hoover to do us a formal appraisal. Written if you want, signed. —Dimmie and me, we were getting together when he left. I knew I could handle him."

"The son...he might really be...I don't know. *Tougher.*"

"Maybe not," Jones said. He spat out a red splinter.

"Do we get to change the name?" Agnes asked. "*Dimmie's Half Off* doesn't make no sense. I mean, Dimmie's like gone, anyway."

"We could change the name," said Doris, the other one, on his right, bouncing in her chair. "Call it 'The Twins,' after us!"

"Yeah, us."

"Except, there's already a '*Los Cuates*,' Doris said. "Two of them. Over on Lomas."

Agnes said, "Could we make *Los Cuates* change it?"

"Give up their name?"

"Buy the name, Daddy! You buy it! *We're* the twins!"

Sanchez shook his head.

Jones ignored them. The girls were pushy, but Eloy Sanchez was the board. The Caucus's annual budget was whatever Sanchez could spare from his own pocket. The Caucus's programs and political goals were what Eloy said they were.

"We'll take over *Half-Off* and run it right," Sanchez said. "Women don't know about running anything."

"Daddy!"

"And they don't know shit about business," Sanchez said, ignoring the twins. "So you go talk to Wince."

"If he won't sell…?" Jones said.

"You mean, if he won't sell…to *you*?"

"Well…yeah."

"That would be a problem."

"I'm doing what I can."

"*Your* problem."

"Well, what if—"

"Make it work."

The girls were smiling now. "You're funny, Daddy," one of them said. The other nodded. Agnes and Doris.

When Leon Quintana showed up with coffee, Wince was perched on the hood of his Mustang. "What's the damage?" Quintana said.

"Take a look." Wince hopped off the hood and pointed. "They smashed the windshield in three places. You can see the impact stars there. Three of them. And check this out." He crouched at the front bumper. "Both headlights, and the right parking light and turn signal."

Quintana ran a hand over the driver's side headlight lens, cracked rough and sparkling in the sunshine. "Not the tail lights?"

"Should I thank somebody for that?"

"I only asked. ... It could have been worse."

"The cops find the son of a bitch who did it, I'll repay his kindness with a tire iron."

"No you won't," Quintana said. "Here. It's Black, no sugar." He handed one cup to Wince and drank from the other. "And they won't find him."

"They won't even look, 'swhat you mean." Wince drank. "C'mon in," he said. "I've got to call the insurance guy."

Wince led the way through the house onto the rear *portal*. After the phone call, they sat in a pair of canvas director's chairs overlooking the rear wall and the fluttering green-gray sweep of the Cardoza vineyard reaching west toward the river.

"My lot stops there, at the wall," Wince said. "But the view is mine all the way to Cardoza's barns. I get to enjoy the vines. I don't have to pick the grapes."

"Life is good."

"Yeah, good. Until some bastard smashed my windshield."

"Maybe he thinks you've got it too good."

"Or maybe it was just some kid, pissed off at the world."

"Where'd it happen?"

"I told you, I was in with the cleaning crew at Sunrise, finishing whatever I could for next week. I came out and found it."

"Somebody knew the Mustang was yours. And where you were."

"Uh-huh."

"So...it wasn't random."

"But it makes no sense, trash my car over nothing."

"So...it wasn't 'over nothing.' Somebody must be pissed at you. Or twisting your arm," Quintana said. "Maybe you wouldn't do something like that, but a lot of people would. If nobody was watching."

They sat in silence, till Quintana said, "You want to tell me about this other arm-twister who's snooping around? The Harvard lawyer."

"Who? I don't know—"

"His name's David. He left me his card and I checked him out. Thomas Jefferson David, Harvard Law, class of ninety-one."

"You know more than I do."

"He wanted an appointment. I don't know what he's got on his mind. I don't even know how he knew to contact me, is he's looking for you. But I thought maybe I ought to find out. Who is he?"

Wince smiled.

"Is this funny?...You want to meet with him?"

"I have."

"Who is he?"

"He's from Las Vegas. He thinks he's going to run a casino for the Navajos at Window Rock. And you can tell him anything he wants to know. He'll misunderstand, to his own advantage.

"Dumb?"

"Nope. Half smart, but optimistic." Then he laughed. "Nothing discourages him."

"Yeah, well…he's got three names, like the prep school he probably went to. That makes him important."

"He's an irresistible force," Wince said, smiling.

"And you're the immovable object?"

"Maybe Rolan is. We'll see. … At least you just brightened my day."

Quintana walked to the edge of the portal and looked out toward the vineyard. "This is another one of your games, right?"

"I don't know what you mean."

"Oh, you know," Quintana said. "*I* don't know what I mean, but you do. Jesus, Robert! Does everything with you have to be so complicated?"

"It seems to work that way."

"Here's what you do. File your insurance claim, get the car fixed tomorrow. For now, go get your chute. We're going jumping." Quintana rose. "Now."

"What if the adjuster's comes over…?"

"He'll take ten minutes.You don't even need to be here. In fact, he'll be amazed if you are. He can check out the car without you.

Wince shook his head. "I want to know who did it. And the cops won't break a sweat trying to find out."

"The adjuster won't either."

"It's his job, isn't it? Save the company a few bucks? Find whoever did it?"

"Are you still thinking about using that tire iron? Look, Bob. You need a break. I'd say let's go up to Chama and do some fishing, but you won't take the time. The next best thing, we'll take the tram, have lunch up top, and jump. It's a simple solution. A jump focuses you and clears out the cobwebs."

Wince shook his head. "Thanks, but a new windshield is top of the list right now."

$ 19 $

"It's six o'clock," Files said into the phone, when Mr. Tedescu answered the call. He sat with his eyes closed. The damn desk lamp was blinding him. He held a ballpoint in one hand, the hotel desktop notepad in the other. The phone receiver was wedged between his shoulder and ear. It was cold.

"Is David still at the Hilton?" Mr. Tedescu said.

"Yeah, I guess."

"What did he accomplish yesterday?" Mr. Tedescu said. "Has he met with anyone?"

Now what? Was Files supposed to admit he didn't know? Or make something up? He took a chance. "Well, you know. Usual stuff."

"What was that?"

Damn! Caught! "Uh, I really don't know, Mr. Tedescu."

"You don't know?"

"Well, I wasn't like…here. I didn't get in till late, and I come to bed. So I won't see him till, like, later today."

"Then why are you phoning me?" Mr. Tedescu said.

"Cause uh…cause you told me to. Every day. Six in the morning, so I set the alarm and…" He was listening to a dead line. He checked his watch. 6:05. Maybe he could get back to sleep. This body-guarding stuff was a pain in the ass. Even without the checking on David part.

124

David woke at 7:00 when the brilliant morning sun found his window and interrupted a dream he couldn't remember. Something about a party. Bright lights and music. No one there he recognized. Except Mr. Tedescu, sitting in a corner.

He took his time in the shower, whistling the whole time. He shaved around his pucker and dressed. Only three days in Beanerville USA. No, two and a half. And he was making progress. He'd checked out real estate sales. A seller's market but not crazy. And he'd gathered a sense of the town's geography.

The streets were numbered in order off of Central: 1st to 2nd to 3rd, pretty standard.

Cross streets were named for states or U.S. presidents or colleges, with some Mexican names thrown in. Mostly alphabetical.

The city was square, in several ways. Bounded by the Sandia Mountains on the east and the Rio Grande on the west, Albuquerque was divided into quarters. Interstate I-40 went east to west and split the city into northern and southern halves. The other highway, I-25, crossed I-40 north to south, creating the east and west sections. Wince's restaurant, or warehouse, or whatever the hell it was, *Dimmie's Half-Off*, sat within a few blocks of the intersection of the two Interstates, the intersection that locals called "The Big I."

Perfect!

Half-Off marked the town center, like the hole in a doughnut.

Couldn't be better. Interstate access from all directions. Great parking. No nearby competition…

On his way down to breakfast, David sang his new shower song: 'location, location, location,' it went. He was still singing it under his breath when the elevator doors split open at the lobby. The waxed lobby floor was made of tan *saltillo* tiles. Broad red and blue and yellow stripes framed the windows. Imitation Mexican. Garish, probably aiming for cheerful.

Then a shadow darkened the mood, a life-size view of Artie Files. Not an hallucination, not a bad dream, but flesh and blood Artie Files in a green running suit, sprawled on a black leather couch like a lizard on a rock.

Files rose and waved. "Mr. Tedescu said I should come stay with you. In case, you know…" He turned sideways and raised his shirt. A shiny black Glock was tucked in the waistband of his sweatpants. Great way to blow your balls off.

"And the Lincoln?"

"I couldn't turn it in at the airport here. Different rental company, you know? So I drove the fuckin' thing back to Vegas. It took two days. Turned it in, and flew back down. You want to give a guess what that cost me?"

"It took you two days?"

"Yeah, 'cause I stopped off in Window Rock, you know, broke up the trip."

"Why the hell…?" David took a breath, ready to say…he didn't know what.

"It's okay. I'm back. And I got us a Caddy from the airport here. It's out front, and I'm here now, and ready to go."

"If you…" And out of nowhere came a gust of patience. Nothing David could do but live with the situation. He was stuck with Files. There was no shedding this leech, that was already clear. And Files did have some sort of access to their hunky boss. That could be useful. David took a breath and reached out to shake Files's hand. "Okay. Skip it. Welcome back."

Files looked puzzled but said nothing.

"Have you had breakfast?" David said, after a minute. Talking to Files was as much fun as he'd expected. Like having an itch you can't reach.

In the Hilton coffee shop off the lobby, Files wasted little attention listening. He sat hunched over his plate and focused on two-handed eating. Not a surprise.

"I'm working on Wince," David said. "Part of my project, the reason I stayed in this jerkwater town."

"Is he the guy where you and the Indians, like, toured his warehouse?" Files dug into his second bowl of chopped fruit and yogurt. "Why him?"

"Working a deal."

"Oh yeah?"

"It's a long story. I'll tell Mr. Tedescu, later."

"What's this Wince got you want?"

"Nothing, it's—"

"I wouldn't waste no time on him."

"You don't know him. I don't know him. What's your—"

"What is he, part Arab, or something? He don't look like those Indian friends of his, and probly he's not a nigger, but you can bet your ass he's not white, either. What the guys in the joint called one of your 'mud people,' you know?"

"That's exactly the kind of comment that..." David waved it off. "Look. When we're around these gomers, try to cool it. We won't be here long, but while we are, I need Wince to trust me."

"For what? He's a—"

"Doesn't matter. You can wait here."

"Wait's ass! Mr. Tedescu says I stay with you wherever you go. Protect you."

"Protect me? Are you up to that?"

Files smiled. "You're lucky you ain't found out...yet. I beat the shit out of the lottery guy, but Mr. Tedescu said let you go. So I did."

"Uh-huh. Okay," David said. "But when I meet with Wince, you watch. Don't help."

Files nodded. "Sure, why not? You want to give me the sugar there?" He pointed and snapped his fingers.

David flinched but managed a smile. "Here you go." A few days, and he could dump the guy and take his plan to Mr. Tedescu without Files getting in the way.

While Files stuffed his face, David scribbled in his notebook. Three pages full of notes, one page left blank for the final piece. Getting over on Wince.

"That does it." Quintana dropped a manila folder atop the pile on the desk. "We could phone a couple of them, maybe tell them we could move settlement up and get them in a day or two early, if you want. Contracts are all done." He patted the pile of folders."

"No, stick to the schedule." Wince said.

"Next Wednesday, then, nine a.m. Garcia's the first one, unit six."

"Six is ready. ... How long's it going to take, each one of them?"

Quintana shrugged. "If they bring a cashier's check and

don't have any strange last-minute demands, it should be half an hour each. At most. I scheduled them an hour apart."

"*Should* be, you said. You mean, unless they bring along a lawyer to mess things up."

Quintana wore a pained look. "That's why I'm here," he said. "To prevent extraneous messing. Besides, any attorney they might bring in has already read the contract and suggested changes, mostly price, you know. And I've got them all here."

Wince pushed back from the table and crossed to the rear window. "Painters are almost finished," he said, "That's it."

"Uh-huh. Time to celebrate. You can—"

"Elliott's working on that. We'll get the crew in when we're done. Throw a party for them. Most of them, anyway. Use the back room at *Half-Off.*"

"Uh-huh. That's your crew. But I'm talking about *you.* A little adrenalin rush. Wind in your face, heart in your mouth, knees flexed, and..." Quintana bounced once and slammed both feet to the floor... "*Down!*"

Wince smiled and looked past Quintana out the window into the rear court yard. The sod had taken well and was showing new growth, lush and green. The apartment units bore shiny brass numbers on their doors. Beyond the parking lot, the sparse hedge screened the alley from view. Looked good. All of it. "Well...maybe."

"Grab your chute." Quintana pointed at the backpack lying in the corner. "It looks ready to go, somebody packed it. Maybe you?"

"Sure, me. I'm not jumping a chute somebody else packed."

"So...? We going or not?"

"The risk means nothing to you?"

"You turning Nancy on me? All of a sudden you start sweating the 'risk?'"

"C'mon!" Wince shook his head. "If we get caught, you get a fine and a slap on the wrist. In fact you'd probably lawyer your way out of even that. Me? One arrest could put me back in the system."

Quintana laughed it off. "Not to worry."

"Yeah, well, I do. I've had all the Santa Fe vacation I need."

Quintana shook his head. "No problem, as long as we don't jump in the forest preserve, or in some park service land. Fun, my man! You need to loosen up."

Wince turned back into the room to answer but a knock at the door stopped him.

The insurance adjuster, clipboard in hand.

Dan Chutters was catching up on paperwork when his desktop terminal dinged for attention. Ringing bell, blinking cursor...the alarm he'd been expecting. The computer's search function had spotted a name, *Robert Wince,* and was beeping the news. Wince had popped his head up.

Chutters opened the computer file and read the police report on his screen. The report filed yesterday, at the public lobby counter downstairs. Not about Wince, but filed *by* him. A person or persons unknown had committed vandalism and trashed Wince's car. Damage in excess of $300. And one phrase in the information raised Chutters' antenna: an *insurance claim* had been filed. Magic words: insurance claim. And "persons unknown."

Could have been Wince himself. How hard was it to smash

your own headlight? Take a monkey wrench and whack it. Two seconds. No witnesses, no one to say you'd done it yourself. Hit up your insurance company. They wouldn't blink at $300. And not even a full $300, but $300 reduced by any deductible in the policy. They'd pay up without a question. It was a slam-dunk.

Except…nobody would go through all the hassle for $300. And Albuquerque wasn't like Cicero, where—Chutters' experience taught him—burning a car you'd insured with four or five companies could finance a career. What else was involved? Could Wince turn this into a big score, like the turquoise jewelry thing?

Chutters printed the report and walked it down the hall.

Sgt. Bonham scanned the printout before passing it back.

"What do you think?" Chutters asked.

"You really want to know, I think I told you to get over this Wince guy. Where'd this come from?" He waved the printout.

"I tweaked the program that scans the daily report files. It can run a search of our data base, looking for viruses, new cookies, unwanted spy-ware, whatever you tell it to look for. I gave it Wince's name."

"What's a cookie?"

"Another kind of spy-ware that—"

"Let it go, Chutters. How long'd that take you?"

"A couple minutes, that's all. . . . You think I'm sloughing off?"

"Who knows? You put a couple minutes to good use, 'stead of this half-assed suspicion, you maybe coulda found Jimmy Hoffa. Or even whats-his-name Al Qaida."

"Sarge—"

"But no, you discovered your guy Wince, he's ready to per-petrate a major felony. Public Enemy Number One...scam an insurance company outta three hundred bucks. Good going you found this crime wave. Only, if it was me, I wouldn't be telling nobody what I found. They might think you got noth-ing important to do."

"If I—"

"So you found Wince planning something, you don't know what. I can promise you, Dillinger's reputation is safe, for now. Even Billy the Kid, he's probably not worried in his grave. Only, I'm going to worry a lot, if you don't *get the fuck back to work!*"

"Okay, Sergeant. I—"

"No more! I don't even want to hear it!" Bonham snatched up a sheaf of papers and waved Chutters out of the room. "Go!"

Chutters stared at his terminal display screen for a full minute before taking a pack of note cards from of his desk drawer. He laid a blank card on the desk, debating. One phone call to the DMV got him the name of Wince's auto insurer, and a phone number. He listed them on the card and spun his chair around, back to the door, before seizing his phone to punch in the number.

$ **20** $

The insurance adjuster hadn't been gone twenty minutes when Files and David appeared, looking for Wince. "So this is what Rolan meant by 'the other place,'" David said, standing in the doorway. "Another construction job. He told me you've got three or four things going at once." He looked around the small office, nodding approval. "Turning a motel into stores, is that it?"

"Sunrise Plaza," Wince said. "Six stores and ten apartments. How're you doing? I thought you might be up in Window Rock. Weren't you and Rolan going to talk with the council?"

"Soon as we can. Meantime, I've been looking around Albuquerque. ... Interesting town."

They shook hands and Wince introduced Leon Quintana.

"Leon and I almost met," David said. "Last week I stopped by his office, looking for you." He shook hands with Quintana. "Tee Jay David. I left my card with your girl."

"Harvard Law, right?"

David smiled. "A generation ago."

"Ninety-one, same year as me," Quintana said. "Only I was here, at U.N.M."

"And...for Law school?"

"That's what I meant."

"Oh." David looked around, seeking an explanation. "So

133

there's a law school here. It's what? Like a night school?"

"No. A regular program." Quintana's smile faded. "With professors, a library and everything."

"Really?" David said. "Well. That's good...

Let me introduce Artie Files. He works for me."

"*For him*'s ass! *With* him," Files said. "Not for him." He nodded at them and backed toward a corner where he stood. A sentry.

"Glad I caught you," David said. "Rolan was telling me, you know your way around Albuquerque, maybe could help me out."

Quintana swept his papers into a pile. "I ought to be going. I—"

"No, no. Stay," David said. "I'm the one interrupting. I can come back later, if...?" He looked from Wince to Quintana.

"Yeah stay, Leon." Wince motioned him to a chair and said to David, "Help you with what?"

"When Rolan and I get going on the casino in Window Rock, the reason I'm in town, I'll need a place to stay," he told Quintana. "It's still months away, but when that project gets underway, I've been thinking, I don't believe I could live fulltime in a little village up there in redskin country, you know?

"What 'village?'" Quintana said.

David shrugged and said, "It's hard to call Window Rock a town."

"Damn straight!" Files said. "Ten minutes and you seen it all."

David snapped a glare at him, and Files leaned against the wall, folding his arms.

"A *pied-à-terre* in Albuquerque would make sense. A place to stay weekends. If I find the right property here, it might be a good investment, now that real estate price's are starting to climb out of the toilet. And Rolan was telling me you'd know some possibilities."

"I've got an apartment to show you right here," Wince said, waving toward the back of the motel. "New, never lived-in, ready to move in. fresh paint and everything. Only eight left, going fast." He looked to Quintana for confirmation and drew a nod of agreement.

Quintana nodded. "Eight left, out of eight."

"Might be an idea," David said, before he recognized that Wince was kidding. "No, really. I'd be happy to take a look. ...And the other units here in front, they're all designed to be little stores?"

"Or offices," Quintana said. "The property's zoned for mixed use, residential and commercial office space, like a dentist's office, or accountant, or doctor."

"We'd even rent to a lawyer," Wince said. "If we could find one who'd pay on time." He looked from Quintana to David.

They laughed, all but Files. David asked about real estate investment opportunities in general, housing prices, the availability of loft space, even showed interest in restaurants. As long as it looked likely he'd be staying in New Mexico, he might look for "not just an apartment but any income prop-erty," he said. "The main thing is potential. Something that'll bring in twelve to fifteen per cent."

"I'm really not up on all that," Wince said. "Leon?"

"Me neither. But I can introduce you to some real estate people."

"No, that's okay," David said. "Just curious. What little I know about Albuquerque, I like. And if I'm going to spend any time here, you know, because of the casino in Window Rock, I want to nose around some."

"Good idea," Quintana said.

Wince watched David as the man talked, curious at this new façade—quiet attention—unlike David's indifference at *Half-Off* only days earlier. "Real estate advice?" Not a chance. The man was probably a good poker player, but even the best have involuntary 'tells'— nodding, or sucking their teeth, or feigning unconcern. Wince couldn't define David's tells, but he knew he was seeing one.

They agreed. Quintana would put David in touch with friends familiar with the current real estate market. "I won't be in my office this afternoon, okay, but call tomorrow, and I'll have some names for you."

Files started toward the door but stopped with an exaggerated sigh when David paused.

"I'm sorry, Wince," David said. "Am I keeping you? You two look about ready to take off somewhere."

"Robert and I are headed up to the crest." Quintana bent down to pick up Wince's pack from the floor. "Takin' a beak."

Files twitched, his first sign of animation.

"Is that a chute?"

Wince nodded but said nothing.

"I been sky diving," Files said. "Three times. Helluva kick. You do that? I wouldn't take you for a jumper."

"Uh-huh, we have," Quintana said. "Both of us."

"What kinda plane you using?"

Wince shook his head. "No plane. It's base jumping."

"I know about that, seen it on Tee Vee," Files said. "How about I go with you?"

David interrupted. "Files means he's interested in—"

"You don't have to talk for me. I already said, I been sky diving. Three times. There's this guy flies out of McCarran Airport, you go to his dorky class in the morning, learn the tricks, jump after lunch. Three times, I went, only now I don't have to do the class each time, 'cause I know all that shit. You can take a camera with you, strap it around your neck when you jump, get some really cool shots!"

Wince smiled. "Base jumping's not much Like sky diving."

"Yeah? It's jumping with a chute, like I already did."

"Sky diving, you jump from a plane. At altitude," Wince said.

Quintana said, "Base jumping's different."

"Uh-huh," Files said. "If you say so. Real different, huh? You jump from a base?" He snickered.

"'BASE' is an acronym. The initials stand for *Building, Antenna, Span*...like a bridge span...and *Earth*." He ticked off the definitions on his fingers. "B,A,S,E. You jump from a fixed point, at a lower altitude than sky-diving, sometimes over rough terrain, or even a city street. There are—"

"You jump from an antenna? That don't make no sense. Antennas are—"

"Okay, Files. Let it go," David said. "It's not antenna like on your house, or car."

"More like broadcast or relay towers, like the ones up on the mountain ridge, you see them lit up at night," Quintana said. "There's one in Poland, over two thousand feet tall. Or there was, till a few years ago. I heard they took it down."

"Okay, I got it," Files said. "How about me and David go with you?"

David shook his head. "We've got work to do, so we'll let you two—"

"Work's ass!" Files said. "I'm goin!"

Wince tried again. "We may not jump today. We're going to take the tram, then look at the jump site, But it depends on the wind, or who might be hanging around. We don't need anyone turning us in. And how we feel when we get there, how—"

"I told you, I already jumped three times. I ain't some green rookie. I don't need any *permission*. Just tell me where can I get a chute."

Quintana tried to take over as they left the office, headed toward their cars parked out front. "You don't want to rush into this," he told Files. "The standard advice is, you start out with sky diving. You take a hundred-fifty jumps, learn to hit a thirty-foot landing zone every time. *Then* you think about base jumping."

"You *think* about it," Wince said. "You still don't do it, not if you're smart."

"You guys did a hundred-fifty sky dives?"

"Me, yes," Quintana said. "Robert took the short cut. He did his fifty, then he—"

"Fifty two," Wince said.

Quintana nodded. "Then he went to Bridge Day in West Virginia last year, and they let him jump the New River Gorge Bridge."

"Jumped off a fuckin' bridge? Into a river?" Files laughed. "Why'd he even need a chute?"

"Eight hundred eighty feet high," Quintana said. "Twelve, thirteen seconds." He smiled. "Eight seconds, if your chute fouls."

They stood beside Quintana's Grand Cherokee and David said, "Maybe we could come observe? Let Files see what it's about and he may get over the idea."

"We're taking the tram up to the crest," Quintana said.

"And we're right behind you," Files said. He led David to the Cadillac and waved. "In," he said.

$ **21** $

Detective Dan Chutters was swamped. Good deal. After resigning from the department in Chicago he'd headed west, caught on here, and diddled away nearly a year on Albuquerque's unfamiliar streets, putting in his time in APD. An apprenticeship, like starting over again. A year on the streets and two citations along the way. One for busting a lay preacher running a pigeon drop on retirees. The other for taking down a stock broker with a car trunk full of hot bearer bonds. And he'd passed the written test that got him a gold shield like the one he'd given up in leaving Chicago. *Detective* Dan Chutters. Again.

In spite of the mayor's campaign promises to bring the depleted department to full strength, APD was short a quarter of its budgeted workforce. For the last six months Chutters had worked without a regular partner, linking up with others only as each case he caught demanded, partners for a day, or week.

But being short-handed had advantages. Without someone to slow him down by debating each move, he'd cleared more than half his pending cases. He cleared them, or decided they'd never be cleared and dumped them into the shit can of his Open Files. Let them rest there, cold cases getting colder, till the brass recognized the futility of trying to *open* them again.

With no regular partner looking over his shoulder, Chutters had time to scratch an itch without explaining himself. Or try out a new place for lunch, half the excuse he used today to head east out Lomas, past the hot bed motels, used car lots and RV dealers. He picked up a Dr. Pepper and a *burrito* at a *Seven-Eleven* and parked outside the old Eastside Motel—*Sunrise Plaza*, the new sign said—to eat. He was there, watching. when Elliott Chávez walked out.

He rolled down his window. "Going to lunch?"

"It's that time," Chávez said. He bent down to face Chutters through the open window. "APD driving Buicks all of a sudden?"

"I am. That piece of crap Crown Vic they gave me died. Fifty thousand rough miles on it, bald tires and a transmission sounds like a coffee grinder. I told them to keep it and I'd drive my own car, till they get me a better one."

"Okay. Good idea." Chávez nodded, pretending interest.

"Is Wince inside there? In the office?"

"He's out somewhere with the lawyer, lunch I think. You want to talk to him?"

Chutters debated, then said, "Maybe you can give him a message for me."

"Sure. What's up?"

"I hear he had some trouble with his car."

"Busted windshield and headlight, that's all. How'd you hear it?"

"Good question. How come I couldn't find an accident report?"

"It wasn't an accident." Chávez shrugged. "Some kids screwing around, I guess. But how did you know—"

"Tell Wince, any time there's paperwork involved, there's a record kept. A file, you understand? Anybody can find out what you're doing, and if what you're into gets your ass in a sling, maybe you shouldn't do it with people watching."

Chávez stood erect and stretched the crick out of his neck. "You got it wrong, Detective. There's no problem here. Bob's minding his own business. The way everybody should do."

"You mean me?"

"Did I say that?"

"Yeah, well maybe it turns into my business, if I find out he's running an insurance scam."

"Jesus, man! What's it take to convince you people. Bob's been straight—"

"I'm not *you people*! I come around to give Wince a tip, there's a lot of ways he could get fucked up again, and you give me attitude. All you need to say is, 'thank you,' and pass it on to Wince. You got that?

"I don't know what you mean, but I'll tell him."

Chutters motioned Chávez away from the car door and climbed out. "And while you're at it, tell him he's got a problem, his new friends."

"What new friends?"

"Cut the crap! These two Vegas guys. One of them's got a sheet on him this long. Assault, grand theft auto, whole string of arrests back east. And the other one probably ought to have. Wince's gotta watch out, hanging with mooks like that. They'll be in the system soon enough. You think Wince wants to go back inside with them?"

Chávez shook his head. "Okay, so Bob made some mistakes, but that was before, and there's no reason you keep busting his ass about…about, I don't even know what. He's too smart to get himself screwed up again. You know that. He works hard, wouldn't give anybody trouble who didn't start up with him first!"

Chutters peered at Chávez. "Was that comment meant for me? You *warning* me?"

"Jesus, Chutters! I'm just telling you Wince is like a boy scout, or a social worker. He's got your back, every time."

"If you say so."

"Yeah, yeah, humor me. But ask Begay, or anybody else who knows Bob."

"Okay. But the *new* friends, these guys from Las Vegas, they're trouble! Tell him." Chutters ducked into his car and slammed the door.

Chávez walked to his pickup, kicked a brick into the street and turned back to glare.

Chutters returned the look but said nothing. He drank from the Dr. Pepper bottle on the seat beside him and watched Chávez till the man drove off.

Now his damn *burrito* was cold!

Tom Jones was beat. It wasn't physical exhaustion, like the sore back and bruised muscles he'd expect from riding a jackhammer or shifting sacks of grain. It was the stress of trying to find work, or to hang onto the job he had, while a dozen other *vatos* thought they could do it better than him. He had to schmooze more than 100 legislators, 70 of them state representatives, and near 50 senators. Then there were the committee chairs, and governor's appointees, some civil service drones who never did squat but demanded respect, and the changing committee memberships. That was just state officials. The federal delegation was even harder to work.

Power moved through the shifting groups like the shadow of a passing cloud. Jones had to know who was 'in,' or on the way in, their wives' names, maybe their anniversaries, a little something about their kids, which ones liked golf (for the fund-raisers he organized, two or three a year). Which ones wanted free Lobo basketball tickets. Who expected Chivas Regal in his Christmas stocking and who'd be content with a case of *Tecate*. He had a computer to help him, of course, but that meant keeping the *pinche* computer files up to date. The pressure never quit.

And some of the would-be power brokers he dealt with, especially the South Valley *vatos*, excluded him. They did it figuratively, by speaking Spanish when he met with them (and he had to pretend to follow everything they said), or directly, by blowing off the meetings he arranged.

That would all change...when he owned his share of *Dimmie's Half-Off*...or whatever Eloy Sanchez decided to re-name the *pinche* place. Jones could manage the restaurant, be respected for what he did, join the Hispano Chamber, take a leadership role in the Caucus, and leave all the ass-kissing to the punk kids who thought lobbying was easy. They'd find out just how easy it was, when Tomas Jones wasn't doing the work of three men for them.

Only one barrier between him and that future: Wince's stubbornness.

That's why he walked into *Half-Off*, carrying a lace shawl for Janie Collier.

"We're closed," Janie said. "We'll be open in a few... Oh.

It's you." She wore khaki Dockers with the knees dirty where she knelt on the floor. She was sticking white letters into slots on a framed cloth message board. It stood leaning against a glass display case and listed the gift items in the case.

"Hi, Janie. How you doing?" He took off his hat. Respect.

"Bob's not here now."

"You expect him any time soon?"

She shrugged and crouched to view the board she was working on. "These letters look even to you?"

"Look fine."

"Darn things. I can't tell the capital 'eye' from the little 'ell,' and the naughts and ohs look alike. What do you think?"

"Yeah, looks good to me. What's it for?"

Jones leaned close to read the list of items, white letters against a maroon background. His gaze jumped from the list to items scattered in the display case, ashtrays, junky looking bamboo tomahawks, plastic turquoise bracelets. "Oh, I get it. You going to put prices on that list?"

"Buck said just the names. People can ask the price, if they see something they like."

"*Buck* said?"

"Buck Tsosie. He's supposed to be running the shop, only I don't know where he got to, either. Bob will be back pretty soon. He's out at the Eastside Motel, helping clean up. You want to talk to him, you could run out there."

"No, not now. I came by to see you, if you want the truth." He gave her his best smile and laid a package atop the display case. "I saw this, and I thought of you right away." He pushed the package toward her.

"Oh yeah?" Janie slid the box of letters off to one side and examined the package. She picked it up, a box in silver wrapping paper, a narrow blue ribbon tied diagonally around the box. She hefted it, checking the weight, and held it up to one ear. "What is it?"

"Open it."

"Why you bringing me presents? I don't even remember you're much of a tipper. Now this, out of the blue."

"Open it up." Jones backed away and nodded at the package, then watched as she carefully untied the ribbon, removed and folded the paper, and lifted the top off the box. She drew out an ivory-colored lace *mantilla*, shook it open and held it up to the light.

"Go ahead, put it on."

She tilted her head and peered at Jones for a moment. "What's on your mind?"

Nothing! Swear to God! I thought you'd like it."

"Uh-huh, yeah, it's real beautiful. Except, where'm I gonna wear a fancy thing like this?"

"When you go out…"

"Okay, Mister Jones," she said, refolding the *mantilla* to lay it back in the box. "First thing I'll do, I think maybe I'll call your wife and thank her for it. How'd that be?" She slid the box toward him.

And he pushed it back, laughing. "You got this all wrong, Janie. Esther knows I'm giving it to you. I tell you what happened. She got this from a mail order place in Mexico, only they screwed up and sent two of them. So I figured, who do I know'd look good in it." He shrugged, smiled again, and held out the box to her. "Nothing else. I'm not hitting on you, or anything like that. Just a gift, 'cause you always been nice to me, when I come in for a cup of coffee or a sandwich. Call it a thank you."

"No reason to thank me. You don't—"

"Or...I can give it to one of the Sanchez twins, only there's two of them, and they—"

"No!" She snatched the box. "Maybe I could wear it." She shook it open and cast it around her shoulders, peering back to examine it. "Kinda of fancy, but you never know..."

"Right," Jones said. "Looks terrific on you."

"It does, now that you say." She turned side to side, checking her reflection in the large front window. "Well...thank you. Umm... can I get you a cup of coffee?"

"I don't know. I've gotta run. But what you could do, tell Wince that I stopped to see him, and we need to talk." He handed her an envelope. "Give him this, okay? And ask him to call me. My number's there in the letter."

"He'll be back this afternoon, I don't exactly know what time."

"Tell him I need to see him." Jones walked out, stopping in the doorway to smile his good by. He watched Janie back against her reflection and admire it. Preening.

Even a casual ally could be useful. Jones left, pleased with himself. Every little bitch helps.

$ 22 $

Mike Baca latched the tramcar door.

The tram operator inside the glass-wrapped base station listened for the okay from Baca's counterpart, who was crewing flight number nine, still high atop the crest. He nodded back, pointed at Baca, and hit the switch to start the take-up drum rumbling as it pulled in the cable. The tramcar at the base of the Sandia ridge danced away from the dock and swung into its climb.

Baca scanned his load of tourists. Usual bunch. As always. No celebrities, no one special in the group. Pale-skinned easterners sweating their way through the Land of Enchantment, cameras in hand and credit cards tucked into an inside pocket, hidden from all the imaginary Mexican pickpockets they'd heard about but would never meet.

"Our flight today will take...oh...say, fifteen minutes. It's non-stop...usually, unless something goes wrong."

He waited.

No reaction. Nothing.

Buncha stiffs! Rotary Club guys, blue-haired old women with sweaters draped over their shoulders. Not wearing them. More like shawls, or little ponchos. Same people, same costumes, every day.

He'd had enough. He had to get another job. His *Tia* Julia was on him about going back to finish school and get a degree

148

in something. Anything. Maybe he would. But for now...

"We'll be traveling two and a half miles, over the world's longest aerial tram line," he said. "We climb—"

"Say what? Longest in the world two miles?"

It was the jock in the sweatsuit. But Baca knew how to handle—

"They got one at the Grand Canyon longer than this."

"No sir," Baca said. "There's no cable car at the grand canyon."

"This guy told me." Loudmouth turned away to convince the others. "Two miles is nothing! The one they got there's at least—"

"Files! Drop it!" The flashy guy in the thousand-dollar suit, the jock's boss of some kind, spoke up. He stared down the jock and nodded for Baca to carry on.

"I'll have to check on that," Baca said. "What I know for sure is..." He spoke up, taking charge again, "We climb from six thousand feet at the base to approximately ten-five at the top. You'll see what I mean." He skipped the rest of his canned speech. Last thing he needed was an argument. No point in trying to work this crowd.

He didn't often see four guys get on his tram together. Mainly families or couples. Once in awhile a pair of climbers, if they didn't drive up the east side. Hikers who came to walk the ridge. Or a marathoner in training here at altitude. In the winter it was half skiers jamming the car on the way up to ski down the east slope, only the 'wounded' coming down this side of the ridge in the tram. But this foursome today...two of them wore backpacks. They might be hikers. And he'd seen the one in the Red Wing trail boots before.

Somewhere... Oh! With the hot Navajo *chica*. —But the other two weren't local. They looked more like L.A. or Dallas—'big city,' not typical tourists, self-important, maybe hard guys.

Baca watched the downward-bound flight swinging toward them at the halfway point where the two cars would meet and pass each other. Same as every trip. Ride up, ride down. —Only three and a half flights to go for the day. He checked his watch.

"Did you hear about Shirley Obee?" Leela stood at the narrow counter in Rolan's kitchen, grating cheese over a wooden bowl heaped with salad greens.

Her brother shook his head. "No mustard?"

"On yours, if you want. Not mine. I don't know how you can eat that. Mustard on everything." She tossed the salad with a pair of large wooden forks. "It's in the refrigerator."

Rolan fetched condiments and said, "What about Shirley?"

"I thought you'd heard by now. She was raped. Somebody roughed her up, and dumped her out by the haystacks."

"Was it somebody she knew?"

"No. They're looking for him."

"Did Shirley describe him, at least?"

"Uh-uh." Leela shook her head. "It wasn't like that. She doesn't remember anything about it. I'm guessing it was rufy, you know, the 'date rape drug?' She can't remember a thing that happened between when she had a Coke at Winston's place, then she woke up near the haystacks."

"Who'd she have the Coke with?"

"She doesn't remember."

"Yeah, that sounds likely." He shook his head. "Having a Coke, only she doesn't know who with. You betcha. If I was Malcolm, I'd want to talk that over." He squirted mustard on his salad.

"I don't know how you can eat that."

"Practice," he told her, with a grin.

"That's all you're going to say?"

"About what?"

"About Shirley. "

"Let's say, she makes too many friends, too easy."

"You're blaming the victim?"

"I'm having lunch."

"And what' we know's been happening back on the rez, that's nothing, huh? I warned you the place would turn bad if we let those Vegas crooks started hanging around."

"Oh God! You back to that? David and his driver, they aren't up in Window Rock. They're staying here in Albuquerque."

"And you've been talking to them."

"Listening, maybe. Look, Leela. You know the casinos are coming. Isn't it better to have some say about them, instead of hiding your head in the sand, till one day it's too late?"

"What do you want me to say?'"

"You can't affect what you don't understand. There's that old saying: 'Keep your friends close. Keep your enemies closer.' You ever hear that?"

Leela pushed her stool away from the counter where they sat. "You're starting to catch on. Calling them the enemy. Maybe you'll recognize David and the Chimp for who they are."

Rolan took a breath. "Will you listen to me? No arguments, just listen."

She nodded and folded her arms. Willing to listen, not ready to be persuaded. Braced.

"Okay. David's been telling me about his experience, and the place that he runs in Vegas. He—"

"*Ran.* He doesn't run it now."

"Okay, 'ran.' *The Shangri-La.* He says if we saw it, we'd understand the kind of operation he could manage for us at Window Rock." Rolan hiked his stool nearer and leaned on the counter. "He's invited you and me to go up to Las Vegas and see his casino there. And the town.

"You know, Las Vegas isn't just about gambling. They call it the 'City of Churches.' And there's a big Mormon temple..."

"You are so gullible."

"Let's go take a look, then we make up our mind about him. And about the casino."

"Why me?"

"I guess David figures, if he can convince you, others will be easy. — Don't underestimate the man, Leela. He's a smart guy. And successful. I think we ought to at least listen to him."

She shook her head, and Rolan redoubled his arguments. In ten minutes he'd exhausted his list of reasons but hadn't moved her. She doubted his summary of David and the man's capabilities, denied that a visit to the casino he'd managed would persuade her otherwise, and spiked every argument Rolan threw up.

"So what do I tell him? You won't even listen? Look at it this way: we take a weekend trip to Las Vegas, let David show you the temptations of 'sin city.' You can resist those temptations and persuade him you mean it. When he knows he'll never get your support, maybe he'll give up his plans."

"Fat chance."

"Somebody has to compromise, or I'm going to go nuts between you two."

She took his hand. "Poor Rolan. Mistreated by his baby sister. ...I'll tell you what. I'll go see this *Shangri-La* with you, if you tell me he's buying the plane tickets."

Rolan hopped off his stool. "Better than that. This man he worked for's got a private jet. He'll send it to come get us. We'll fly up Saturday morning, stay at *Shangri-La*, come back Sunday night. Okay? Can I tell him you'll do it?"

"If Robert comes along."

"Robert?" Rolan slumped again. Nothing was easy with her. "What's he got to do with it?"

"One more in the plane won't matter."

"Tee Jay wants to talk to *us*. This is about a *Diné* casino."

"David will only try to manipulate us, and I'd like Robert there, to referee. Will you ask him to come with us?"

"Aren't you the one always telling him to lighten his load and stop overdoing things? He's tied up with..." He saw her clenched jaw and shrugged. "Me getting caught between you and David isn't enough. Now you want Robert in the middle, too."

$ 23 $

Two miles west of the Sandia crest, toward the distant mesas and their black-rimmed volcanic craters, a pair of hot air balloons drifted above the Rio Grande. Both balloons were made up of alternating red and green panels, brilliant against the milky blue sky. "See 'em?" Quintana said. "Maybe two thousand feet high."

"There's another one up that way. What is that...north?" David pointed upriver at a mustard-colored balloon, smaller, almost colorless in the distance.

Quintana nodded. "North. In October, at the balloon fiesta, there's five hundred of them in the air at one time. You ought to see it. The sky's full, from downtown all the way up past Bernalillo...the little town you see there."

Wince nodded. "And that's the smart way to start base jumping," he told Files. "Not up here on the crest, but from a balloon. You get a few more seconds more air under you and take a controlled jump from the basket. It's a lot easier than diving off the ridge. Less chance of going head-down. And safer."

"That how you do it? Off a wussy ballon?"

Wince nodded. "You get to pick your landing zone."

"*Oooooh!*" Files faked a shiver. "And it's not so scary."

David said, "Knock it off, Files."

Wince laughed. "No, he's right. Scary's the right word.

154

First-jump jitters, they call it. Another first timer with me at Bridge Day got scared and wet himself on the way down."

"Shit! I jumped from a whole lot higher than eight hundred feet."

David said. "That's his point. 'Higher' is what you did. Lower takes balls."

"Well, they going to jump or not?"

The four of them stood beside the split rail fence that bordered the ridge-top trail. Quintana and Wince carried their chutes looped over one shoulder, like packs. The other loop and chest strap hung free. Wince scanned the trail behind them and saw no one. No one on the trail ahead.

"Maybe," Quintana said. "Take a look." He pointed ahead toward a bend where the trail disappeared beyond a clump of bushy junipers. A fresh breeze plucked at the branches and dusted the air with wafted yellow pollen. He ducked and led the way.

And while they walked, Wince described a base-jumper's rig. He offered details both Files and David, but only David listened. Files marched ahead, striding away from them.

"A seven panel chute, wider than long. A pilot chute forty inches or more in diameter and what they call a 'slider.' It's a mesh cage to keep the lines from tangling as the chute deploys. You've only got four seconds to gain velocity on the jump before you toss out the pilot chute. When you're falling fast enough, it catches air and pulls the main chute open."

"Three or four seconds?"

"By then, you're falling at fifty-plus miles an hour, and you've only got a dozen seconds till you hit the ground. Two breaths and...*wham!*"

David said, "Not for me. I'll stick to seven-card stud and a good cigar, not playing paratrooper. You've got more nerve than I do."

"Maybe. Probably not enough to play poker with you."

"You play?"

"Nothing to brag about. You'd clean me out in an hour."

"Yeah, I see." David peered at him. "You wouldn't be hustling me, would you?"

"Hey! You two coming?" Files stood in mid path, hands on his hips, shouting.

They caught him and turned the corner to see Quintana, poised half way out to end of a twenty-foot shale shelf that pointed west into space. Wind from the west snapped at his pants and mussed his hair. He pointed at the valley floor below, leaning against the wind as he sidled closer to the edge. The valley held a jumble of automobile-size boulders surrounding a grassy patch that sloped away from them toward the city suburbs and the river. The patch looked very small. An asphalt roadway curved away from the city streets below, past a pair of tennis courts and ended at a grassy area.

"Small enough," Wince said. "Seventy, eighty feet wide, not much when you're bearing down on it in mid-air. About the size of the Northside Tennis Courts you can see to the west. Maybe like a carrier deck looks to a jet pilot."

Quintana nodded. "That's the spot. Hit that flat area, the grassy area there or the tennis court, you walk away. Miss it, and they take you home on a stretcher. Or in a rubber bag."

Files walked nearer the edge to peer down. "Shit!" He turned back to face them. "What you want to bet I couldn't do it?"

"Files! Get away from the edge!" Hesitant, David took a step forward.

Files laughed. "Gets to you, does it?" He whirled to tell Quintana. "Do it! Let's see you jump."

Quintana and Wince shared a glance, and Wince snatched up a handful of grass to toss in the air, checking the wind. The grass flew back in his face, and he shook his head. "Not today," he said. "I'm going back."

"Shit!" Files spun on his heel and started back down the trail, muttering.

Quintana nodded and said, "Another time." He stepped off the ledge and started back toward *High Finance*, his chute still swinging from one shoulder by a single strap.

"I'm checking my chute," Wince said.

"That's cool." Quintana nodded. "Leave 'em both in the changing room locker." He spun his chute off his shoulder and carried it swinging in one hand.

"What's that mean, check it?" David asked. "Where?"

"Half the people who come up here skiing leave their street shoes in one of the lockers at *High Finance*. It's not a checkroom, more a place to change and leave your gear when you stop for lunch. In there." Quintana pointed at the lower level of the restaurant and followed Wince down the wooden steps.

"Be right back," Wince said.

Files walked away past the restaurant, bitching the whole way about people who talk a good game but chicken out when crunch time comes. "Now we gotta wait for the cable car?" he said.

"Don't worry about it," David said.

Quintana rejoined them, empty-handed now. "There's a back way off the ridge. Right there." He indicated a gravel road that snaked its way east down the backside of the mountain.

"Then let's drive down, get the hell out of here."

"Did you bring a car up with you?" Quintana said.

"The tram's on the way up." David tried calming them.

"So we wasted half the day coming up here." Files turned away, muttering. "Pussies!"

Wince tuned him out.

They waited to board the downward-bound tram.

Files pulled David aside. "Now what?" he said. "We waste half the fuckin' day, then chickenshit Wince backs out. I think he never jumped at all. I told you he's full of it. Why you sucking up to him now? He's got squat to do with that Window Rock place. If Mr. Tedescu knew you was—"

"Knock it off!" David motioned Files back along the path toward the restaurant and away from the tram loading dock. "I know what I'm—"

"And I'm getting sick of this whole place. I got my own life, you know. Chasing buncha cowboys and Indians around ain't it. You get your job done here, we can go back where we belong."

"You belong where I put you."

Files stared at David, choked, pointed at him and started to laugh. "Where *you* put me? *You*? You're nothing! I took down three guys already, any one of 'em could break you in half without trying. Only thing keeps you whole is Mr.

Tedescu needs whateverthehell you're doing for him." He laughed again. "*You!*"

David almost whispered. "Just keep it down," he said, glancing at the loading dock. "It's simple. I'm buying Wince's restaurant, but he doesn't know it yet."

"A restaurant! —So he won't sell, so what? Let's finish up and head back. Mr. Tedescu can—"

"He *will* sell. I'll make it happen. That motel is going to break him. He needs to unload the restaurant, just to get well. But it might take time to persuade him. If I—"

"I'll 'persuade' his ass! Let me talk to him. I can—"

"That's exactly what I *don't* need. I'm talking finesse, not broken bones. Your job is, do what I tell you."

Files clenched and opened his fists, turned to look at Wince. He stood tapping a toe, almost bouncing in place. When he turned back he was calmer. But not much. "How long's this 'finesse' gonna take? I want to get the fuck outa here!"

David drew a silver money clip out of his pocket and jerked loose a fifty. "Here," he said. "We get down below, take the Caddy, go get yourself a good steak and a couple drinks. Let me work on Wince. I'll get this wrapped up soon. Trust me."

"Uh-huh. Trust you." Files's anger turned to sulking but he took the money. "Where'm I gonna get that 'good steak' in this burg, huh? Tell me that."

David slapped Files on the shoulder. "Just hang in there. Things are working out fine. When we get this done, Mr. Tedescu's going to be real pleased with both of us. I'm doing it for him. We'll both come out of this looking good. Just cool it for now."

"Sure, I'll cool it." Files shook his head. "*Cool it. ...* Dumb shit!"

Jones had run out of time. Eloy Sanchez's orders said either get Wince to accept an offer on *Half-Off*, or Sanchez would take over the negotiations. No more dicking around.

When Jones pushed through the motel's main door, he saw Elliott Chávez peeling masking tape off the broad front window and scrubbing the glass with a dripping sponge. "*Hola Chávez. ¿Qué tal?*"

"*Nada. ¿Y tú?*"

Jones only mumbled.

"What'd you say?"

"Nothing...Wince here?"

"D'you see him?" Chávez directed Jones's gaze around the office. The scrap lumber and broken drywall had been cleared away, the floor swept and mopped. The rear window sparkled, and Chávez picked up a squeegee, ready to attack the front window.

"D'you know if he got my note?"

"You two passing notes, now? Maybe you could catch him after study hall."

"C'mon, Chávez. I sent him a note, an offer, really. The people I represent want to buy his old restaurant. Dimmie's place, you know? It's just sitting there, and we could restore it. We made him a good offer, and we need an answer."

Chávez laughed. "You guys, you never give up. Don't you know Bob by now? He's not going to sell."

"That's bullshit! He'll sell."

"You think you can make Bob do something he doesn't want to, you got the wrong guy. He did almost two years in the joint without breaking a sweat and came out hard as a hammer. Don't think 'cause he's quiet, he's some wimp."

"What happens if he can't pay his bills? How tough is he gonna be, broke?"

Chávez shook his head. "You don't want to find out."

"It's coming. I know some things."

"Sure, and I know he's not here. So you can take off."

Jones backed to a chair and sat down. "I'll wait for him. ... You know, you could help us out.

I mean, why not? You're Hispano too, man. You're one of us. You know the way people like Wince screw us over. You—"

"Get the hell out of here!" Chávez grabbed Jones's arm and hauled him to his feet. "Out!"

Jones stumbled to the door. "Wake up, Chávez! You're making a mistake, man! We're buying the *pinche* restaurant, and you're better off helping than getting in the way!"

"Uh-huh. Out!" Chávez pushed him out the door and slammed it after him.

Jones walked back to his car to wait for Wince.

Wince watched the tramcar swaying toward them. Only eight people on the platform with him, waiting for the downward bound flight. That's what the billboards along I-25 that Wince saw every day called it. A 'flight,' not a 'ride.' Files was still muttering about chicken-shit pussies who welsh on their promises. Quintana was cranky about something, too. Only

David stayed quiet, controlled and observing.

"Better be getting back" Wince said. "I can't dump all the work on Elliott."

"Is that Chávez, your partner?" David said.

"Or I'm his. For two years now," Wince said. "Elliott knows construction better than I do. He was the one who put our crew together. He recruited all these guys he worked with before and knew."

"But it was you hired them."

"We did it together."

David mulled over his next comment, chewing his lower lip Wince enjoyed watching him. The conversation couldn't be hurried. Wince could wait. The pitch he saw coming had to be David's idea. David had to offer it, at his own pace.

"You've got a lot of partners," David said. "Quintana's another one, right?"

"Kind of, yeah, on the motel conversion. All the legal business."

"And Tsosie?"

"The gift shop. You met him there. Why're you so curious?"

"I hear you're looking for another property. Like I am." David turned to face down-slope. He shielded his eyes from the westering sun and rocked from heel to toe, casual. But his left hand was clenched in a fist. Wince saw the tell. The man was not so controlled after all. His question mattered.

Wince let David side-step a half circle till Wince had his back to the other passengers. David grew confidential. "Is that right?" he said. "Another project?"

"Maybe. But it's nothing special, just a long-term thing.

Elliott and I have been looking at a couple of adobes I could play with. Some place on a stream or a lake."

"A lake? In New Mexico?" David waved at the sweep of arid hills climbing to the west horizon.

"You're right, it's not Minnesota, but I think I found what I wanted."

"Well, good luck with that." David paused, thoughtful, cautious. "I've had an idea that might work out for both of us. I told you, I've been looking to pick up a property to develop. If I can find the right one. And you'd probably like to unload some excess baggage. Generate some funds, a cushion let's say. Maybe we can work something out to help both of us." David turned on a big smile.

Too big.

"What do you have in mind?" Wince said, stirring the air with one hand to hurry David along. He pointed at the tram-car swaying on the cable and creaking its way into the loading dock. "We've got to get going." He felt David circling the bait so he twitched the line. "I don't think I know what you mean."

David hesitated. "Think this over, will you? It's your call, I know...up to you. But I might be interested in taking that old restaurant off your hands. *Half-Off*, d'you call it? Investment for me, some ready cash for you. To help finish the other projects you've got going. Maybe that adobe place you mentioned. If we could agree on terms."

There! Wince felt David's interest but held him off. He shook his head. "It's not ready yet. I want to finish the gift shop, first," he said. "It'll be worth more, with that done." And then he set the hook. "*If* I decide to sell."

David laughed easily. "Yes, I see that'd be better. For you. Not so much better for the buyer."

Wince waved a hand. "It's not up to me.

Check with Buck."

"Tsosie?"

"My partner, remember?"

"You don't mind if I talk to him?"

"Didn't you meet with him and Rolan?"

"We talked about his family. You know the kind of stories he tells."

Wince shrugged. "I don't think he' interested in selling, either. So…not much point in chasing after him," he said. "He's tougher than I am."

"C'mon, c'mon!" Files motioned the cablecar closer. "We shoulda drove up here."

The tramcar jolted into the loading dock. Wince and David backed away to give the new arrivals room to exit.

Files crowded closer to board first.

"Let's do it!" he said, pushing past them. "Hop on the bus."

Wince stepped back to let the others enter first. He nodded at the boy running the tram. 'Something' Baca. The ride down…no, the *flight* down, would give David another chance to formulate an offer. And for Wince to listen.

$ **24** $

Wince watched Leela Begay enjoy the hour-plus flight from the Albuquerque Sunport to Vegas. He also saw her try to hide her enjoyment, face stern, her jaw clenched with obvious resolve. The flight was smooth. The corporate jet was sleek and quiet. Leela sat just as quiet, freezing out T.J. David, ignoring his forced pleasantries. She did answer Rolan's comments but initiated nothing. She sat in her rear-facing seat across from Wince and watched the drifting clouds below. Patches of desert, then a glimpse of Lake Mead, flickered through gaps in the clouds. The view softened her resolve, and a smile betrayed her.

"Nice?" Wince said, indicating the cloud layer. "Like snowdrifts."

The drone of the twin jets changed pitch and became a muted hum. The plane lurched into its descent.

The drop brought Leela back. She sat erect again, smile gone. "How much longer now?"

"A few minutes," David said. "Not long. It depends on air traffic into McCarran."

"This sure beats the bus," Wince said. "I could learn to like this."

"Me too," Rolan said.

"Don't get to like it too much," Leela said.

Rolan leaned over to inhale the aroma of the leather seat

165

beside him and smile. "Like a new car," he said. "You pay extra to get this smell at the car wash. They stick a square of cardboard under the floor mat—

"Uh-huh. When all you have to do is buy a million dollar airplane upholstered in dead animal skin and smell the seats."

"Three point two million," David said. "You get nothing air-worthy for one mil anymore."

"Rolan?" she said.

Rolan shook his head. "I'm just making conversation."

"You're too easy," Leela said. "One whiff of power and you go all soft and gooey. What's going to happen to you when you see those pretty neon lights down there, up close?" She pointed out the window.

"I'm looking forward to it. That's why we're here."

"Why *you're* here." She turned to David. "All part of the seduction, isn't it?"

"C'mon, Leela," Rolan said. "Keep an open mind, remember? You agreed."

"Oh, I'm totally open. I'll admire The Strip, openly, and the Fremont Street Experience, and topless waitresses, and slot machines in every gas station and drug store, and maybe a wedding chapel or two. It's the essence of Las Vegas! And hustlers in silk suits selling you shiny plastic chips to play with." She turned her glare on David…and his silk suit.

Rolan looked a plea at Wince, who only shrugged.

"I'm just along for the ride," Wince said. "A neutral observer."

Leela jerked her seatbelt tight.

David peered out the window as the plane dropped landing gear with a grinding racket and dipped into the broken cloud layer masking the oasis below them.

East of Grants, I-40 streaks through a thousand acre patch of crumbled lava spilling off the granite ridge north of the highway, a pitch-colored cover on the land. Pre-historically slick-shiny black, the lava flow had come to resemble the fading porous asphalt of a country road. Now the terrain lies broken by millennia of wind-seeded desert plants—creosote, chamisa, piñon and juniper. It sweeps up toward Mount Taylor, mounded and undulating. In spots it's overgrown with waving grasses. The area is alive with grazing rabbits and the coyotes that hunt them.

One of those spots was a wide depression thirty feet off the interstate, where a State Police cruiser, aimed west, sat half-concealed from passersby. Artie Files ignored it when he flashed past at 90 mph. Cop car sitting there, looked empty. For the moment he didn't know that the trooper inside the car reading his radar gun had only to radio the pair of troopers in their supercharged Firebird parked in the bare-dirt median a mile farther west. He found out after topping a small rise in the highway, when his rear-view mirror showed him the Firebird fishtailing onto the interstate behind him in a plume of dust.

He hit the brakes and flinched at the squeal of his own tires. The Caddy slowed to 70 mph. Too late.

That damn Firebird could move!

Files knew the drill. He pulled onto the shoulder and reminded himself. Cooperate. Be cool. Don't piss off the man.

He had the rental papers for the Caddy and his driver's license in his hand, the driver's-side window down, and a neutral expression in place when the trooper walked up to the car. Two professionals doing a job, they conducted their business with little conversation. Files watched in his rear-view mirror while the trooper in the Firebird checked out car and driver on his dash-mounted computer terminal. No worry. Files had no current warrants pending. The rental was legal. The whole process cost him nothing but a little time, irritant enough, and a fine he'd never pay.

Ten minutes later Files was back on the road toward Gallup and Window Rock beyond. A quick visit to check on that bitch squaw, then head back to Albuquerque. He tossed the crumpled citation out the window and managed to hold his speed below 70 mph for two or three minutes before pushing back up to 90. Then 100.

David stood six feet from the glass-topped table/desk, trying to read upside down, while Mr. Tedescu—swaddled in blue, today—ran a forefinger down a column of five-digit numbers. The week's total net take from the ten penny-slots in the foyer off the lounge was $ 119,450. Ten slots, each netting an average of $11,945. From where David stood, **$11,945**, upside down, spelled **shell**. Wonderful! Number words.

He imagined more. The number **919**, inverted, would read **bib**. And **5909** was **bobs**. That turned **919 5909** into **bobs bib**. David tried to spot others, but Mr. Tedescu's finger moved so fast over the numbers it was tough to read the list.

Standing here, waiting his turn at Mr. Tedescu's attention, David had little else to do. He considered Mr. Tedescu's outfit for the day—almost different, this time—and decided there must be some subtle difference between sky-blue and powder-blue. He didn't know what it was.

He leaned back to look down and and check under the table. There they were. Blue patent leather shoes. Powder or sky?

He checked his watch. Begay and his sister were out there somewhere on their own, beyond David's control. He wanted to get back to them.

"Through in a minute," Mr. Tedescu said.

David tried rotating his head to read the numbers right side up but his neck wouldn't turn far enough. He was still straining to read when Tedescu took the sheet of figures and fed it into the chattering shredder behind him.

"All right," Mr. Tedescu said, squirming ujpright on his throne. "Tell me. Can you make it work?"

The casino. "Yes sir, no problem."

"You won't mind if I doubt that."

"Well, I… Can I ask you, why?"

"Six months ago I sent in an experienced four-man survey crew."

"Yes, you said."

"The same four who did the feasibility study in Bayamon and came back all smiles. Because of them, the new Puerto Rico casino's a go. But they couldn't make a dent in Window Rock. The numbers work fine, but the Indians said no. Four experts couldn't move them. You expect me to believe that you turned them around?"

David looked for a place to sit, knowing there was none. "Umm…not exactly. Not just yet. But I think I can. I'm *sure*

I can! That's why I brought Begay and his sister here, to show them what we've got going. Show them the *Shangri-La*. Persuade them. Did the survey crew try that?"

Mr. Tedescu examined his fingernails and bit one. "No, they did not."

"Well I think that could be the difference.

Their tribal government is ready to listen, and this Begay is someone they'll listen to. The Begays are like a major family in the tribe. He's got relatives till hell won't have 'em. Hundreds of them! We get somebody named Begay fronting for us, we're halfway in already."

"And...his sister?"

"Well, she'll come around. It'll take a little...work, but probably worth it. Navajo women have their own kind of authority. The women are the ones who own the property. The house, the land, everything but the pick-up. They're like the power behind the scene. Begay's sister is tough and probably smarter than he is. If she sees what we've got going here, she'll know what a casino on the reservation could do for her...I think."

"You mean you hope."

"Okay, yes sir. I hope."

"I want to meet them."

Meet them? It came right out of nowhere. Mr. Tedescu never met anyone, not that David could remember, and now...

"Is that a problem?"

"Uh...No sir. No problem.

"And the other one who came with you? Wince?"

"Umm...yes?" David really needed to sit down. "I...uh, I don't think I mentioned him."

"Files did. And this 'Wince' is listed on the plane's manifest. —It *is* my plane, Tee Jay. My pilot." Mr. Tedescu pouted his disappointment with David's naivete. Of course he would know.

"Wince is her boy friend, humping her I'd say, that's all."

"But you've been spending time with him, I hear." Tedesco took out a small nail file and attacked the ragged nail.

"I told you, he'll help us." What the hell had Files been telling him? "Just another way of getting to Begay. Wince is Begay's friend, and his sister's friend. That's it." *Damn Files!*

"Is there any point in negotiating with Wince?"

"Only to work him. He can help us with the girl."

"Files says the man's pussy-whipped. The Indian snaps her fingers, Wince jumps."

"Maybe. But if Begay can't bring his sister around, Wince can."

Mr. Tedescu nodded, considered something, then nodded again. "Is Wince willing to help?"

"I'm working on him."

"To get through to the Begay girl."

"Yes sir." David watched, and nothing happened in Mr. Tedescu's eyes. "Help with the girl," he said again.

"Why would he do that?" Mr. Tedescu asked. "What's his edge?"

"No, no, no. No edge. He's a small-time putz. Like a carpenter. He's got himself in over his head. He's so screwed up right know, he can't tell if he's coming or going. His business is right on the edge of going belly-up."

"If he's not some dumb kid, he probably has advisors. A lawyer, an accountant, so on."

"A lawyer? Sure, but only this local gomer, went to cowboy college, maybe night school. He's nothing."

"That's as may be. But I wonder—"

"Wince is getting crosswise with the girl. The cops are on his case about some old beef he had… Right now he doesn't know his hat from his ass."

"That's not an answer," Mr Tedescu said. "Why would he help you with the girl?"

"I let him think he's helping her, not us."

"Cute. Only…be careful with your pronouns, Tee Jay. It's *you*, he might be helping, not 'us.' He doesn't know there *is* an 'us,' does he? I'm not involved." "No sir." Fucking hunky! Not involved? Wait'll he learns what he missed with his "not involved." David waited, fidgeting. He checked his watch. Time was wasting. Rolan and the others were on their own, picking up who knew what kind of misunderstandings. David had to get to them, take them on the tour he'd designed. But here he stood trading vague speculations with this powder blue hunky. He had to get back to the action in the casino downstairs.

"Bring them up," Mr. Tedescu said.

"They may be busy with—"

"Tonight. I'll meet them." Mr. Tedescu spun his chair left and scanned the wall-mounted display screens. One hand waved goodby.

Dismissed, David went looking for Begay.

$ **25** $

Almost a cocoon, *The Shangri-La* insulated its patrons from the world outside. Like other casinos, it had no windows. At least none that Wince could see. And no clocks. Yard after yard of green and purple carpet reached from one cream-colored wall to another, a gaudy background for the gaudier flashing, blinking, ringing slots.

Wince followed along as David took him and the Begays on a walking tour of the casino main floor. Players at the slots shared a common look, intent on the clangorous flash of spinning lemons and berries and stars and horseshoes whirling past their eyes. Every half-minute a machine some-where nearby paid off with ringing bells and the recorded clatter of imaginary coins announcing a win.

Slots here no longer spewed coins into the bin at the play-er's waist. Most of them displayed the win in LED numerals on a screen at eye level. But real coins or electronic promises, each win brought a shout of celebration from the players, some with a dirty cotton glove on their pulling hand, a few clutching a plastic bucket half-full of nickels…or quarters… or dollars. They all turned envious glances on the winner and went back to feeding the hungry slots.

Beyond the rows and ranks of noisy slots, six blackjack tables formed an island near the Koval Lane entrance in a pit located to snag showroom-bound players when they passed by.

"No more than a twenty-foot straight path anywhere in the place," David said. "Floor layout's crucial. Like at any smart retailer's. You make the customers walk through the merchandise. Every twenty feet they hit a dead end, turn into another row of slots, or an aisle that funnels them to keno or the craps bank, over there." He pointed out another island, this one busier with knots of players gathered at the craps tables, cheering on the shooter, itching for their own turn at the dice.

Waitresses in pushup bras and three-inch heels circled the players, offering free drinks and expensive smiles.

David walked them past *pai gow* tables and roulette wheels, described the noisy side room where Texas Hold'Em attracted the morons who thought an hour watching celebrity TV made them expert enough to join the game. Beyond that was the muted baccarat room where each dealer affected a British accent authenticated by his tux and wing collar.

"All this high style dreck is frosting on the cake," David told them. "People who come here like the glitz, but the casino lives on take from the machines. Let me show you."

He stopped and leaned against the electronic poker machine at the end of a long, jangling row of slots. "In the hottest places, guest rooms go for three, four hundred a night. Dinner in the show room? Forget the three-ninety-nine buffet you see advertised on the buses. A good meal, at a good table, with Celine Dion on the stage, will cost you a hundred and a quarter a head, plus drinks. Show tickets are topping a hundred bucks for acts that used to be free in the lounge. And so what? All that, added up, represents only thirty-five per cent of the casino's gross. Slots are *sixty-five per cent!* You don't need to feed them or entertain them, or park their cars. If you can get players seated in front of the slots, a drink in one hand, you're golden!

"And you can stick two dozen slots in a room the size of a double-wide trailer, give the gomers tugging the handles a hot dog and a beer, and gross over twenty thousand...*a day!* In that one room.

"As long as the people keep coming—fifty million losers a year—the money never stops. They think they're here to enjoy all the glamour. They're really here to feed bills into machines like this baby." He slapped the poker machine, then pointed at the blackjack players hunched over their cards.

"You see how much they're all enjoying themselves?" he said, indicating the players nervously shuffling their stacks of chips. "That's why they're here. For the fun of it."

"Enjoying themselves?" Leela shook her head. "You see anyone with a smile?"

"The lounge never shuts down." He pointed toward the sound of a piano. A woman sang just out of sight beyond the ripple of a hanging beaded room divider. "The dancers keep their tips but they pay us stage rent, each one of them, twenty a twenty-minute set," he told them. "Nickel here, a dime there, it adds up. And the bar generates close to six hundred dollars an hour, that's well drinks, not the prime stuff."

Rolan perked up. "Six hundred net?"

"Gross, but that's twenty-four seven, not just happy hour. —I'll show you a balance sheet later. Let me take you to school."

They pushed through the queue waiting at the entrance to the buffet.

Rolan tapped Leela's arm. "See how busy it is?"

"The entire population of Window Rock wouldn't make a line this long."

"That's the point," David said. "The casino will bring a whole flock of new customers to town. All of them dropping cash on the local economy."

"If you say so."

The cashier's cage had three windows open, with players waiting at two of them. "Cashing in chips," Rolan said.

"Or buying more."

"That's what we'd be hoping." Rolan turned to Wince. "What do you think of the place?"

"I thought they'd impress us with glitz and glamour, like the humongous palaces along the strip—pyramids, canals and sailing ships, rocket launching pads, you know... Disneyland gone nuts. But small and slick is interesting. A pocket-size casino."

"The guest rooms are nice. "

"David gave us a suite. Not a hotel room."

"Sure. So would I, if I was in David's shoes. —What d'you think it'd cost to build a place like this?"

"In Window Rock?"

"That's why we're here," Rolan said.

"I'd guess at least twenty thousand a room," Wince said.

"Come on!"

"No, really. The papers say that Steve Wynn spends eight or ten times that much. But I don't think you need to worry about it. David will bring the money. Just be sure you get a fair percent of the gross."

"What are you telling me?"

"Gross! If you agree to a net deal, you won't See a dime. There'll never be any net."

"Oh c'mon! It's business. I know how—"

"Look, Rolan. Expenses you never heard of will soak up the gross. Consultants, licensing fees, maintenance contracts, contingencies. Whoever keeps the books can find lots of sinkholes for any profit."

Rolan glanced aside at David, leading them to what he called the 'school.' "You think David would screw me?"

Wince tried not to laugh. "Only if he can."

Rolan did laugh. "I know. — Will you be there to remind me about all this when he makes his pitch?"

"This is a *Diné* thing, not up to me."

"Come right in here." David ushered them through an archway off the main floor into a room that held four gaming tables, each one a different game. At the moment, only one of them was busy, the craps table, surrounded by a handful of sunburnt tourists and a woman in a sequined sheath.

"Hey there, Mr. David. How are you?" sequins said. "Are you back?"

"Go ahead, Louise. We're just looking around. Mind if we listen in?"

"Hey, you know the games better than I do." She turned to the people gathered around her table. "It was Mr. David's idea to start a school for new gamblers. Ninety percent of the people you see out on the floor are in Vegas for the first time.

Would you believe that? And Mr. David thought we should make them comfortable, you know? Teach them the games so they'd know what they were doing. I walk them through Blackjack, *pai gow* poker…all the table games. Keno and the slots teach themselves. If you ever played bingo, you can handle keno without my help."

"Louise does a great job."

"Thank you, Sir!" Her nod was almost a curtsey. "We want people to have fun. You know, in the long run you're going to lose. But if you let me give you some advice, you won't lose too much. What you do is, you decide how much you want to spend on a night's entertainment, and stick to that limit. Say you decide on three hundred dollars…"

"Or maybe twenty," Leela whispered to no one.

"Three hundred dollars, you'd spend that on dinner and a show."

"Okay, twenty-five."

"I can't really give you advice, but I can tell you what I do." Louise pointed at the table. "There are a dozen propositions in craps that attract the most play. You do what you want, but I'll tell you, I only play four of them. On these four bets, you can reduce the house's edge to less than two per cent. Cut the odds down, have a hot streak, you can come away with some money in your pocket. Let me show you. It's really all about managing your funds."

She explained both taking and giving odds, the folly of betting on hard-way options, in general summarized craps in ten minutes.

Her audience listened, and watched…all but those antsy to get to the tables and test the lessons just learned. A few of them asked for examples. One woman in denim took notes.

The session was winding down when a man in a black suit and tie walked in. "Hey, David, what are you doing here? I saw you on the floor."

"Hello, Fred. Just visiting. Showing some friends—"

"Shag it!" The man hooked a thumb toward the door. "Out."

"Look, Fred, I was—"

"You know the rules. You're on the commission's list. Somebody sees you here, after that lottery thing, they'll shut us down."

"Okay! I'm gone! *Jesus!* That was a slip-up, a mistake. One mistake…you'd think I'd—"

"Now!" The man seized David's arm and pushed him toward the door. "The back way."

"No! We're going to eat." David jerked free. "Rolan, I'll meet you all at the buffet," he said. "Let me go with Freddie here and straighten things out." He followed the man out.

The silence lasted a full minute. Wince thought it was longer.

Finally, Rolan said, "Hungry?"

Wince and Leela looked at him. At each other.

"Why not?" Leela said. "And David will be joining us?" Rolan nodded.

Leela smiled. "I'm looking forward to it."

$ 26 $

Files's trip was a waste of time. Mostly. More than two hours on the road to get . . . what? Shirley wasn't there when he stopped by Obee's house. Malcolm was pissed about something and didn't want to talk. After ten minutes of getting nowhere, Files sat in the cane-back chair and sucked at the luke-warm coffee Malcolm handed him.

That's when Shirley came in from the kitchen or somewhere in the back of the house. She was wearing a heavy padded robe, swaddled up like an old woman wrapped in a blanket, and she looked at the floor when she talked. She had a big ugly scab on her chin and marks on her forehead. She must of tripped and fell down when Files pushed her out of the car.

Malcolm ranted about some guy must of beat her up. Files knew it wasn't him. A little tap on the jaw, maybe a push in the back. Nothing that'd mark her up like this. After he dumped her out by the road somebody else must of come along and did the rest.

"That's a damn shame," Files said. "No idea who it was?" He peered to see if she remembered any particulars. Most likely she didn't. Maybe she did but was smart enough to keep her mouth shut. Malcolm wouldn't like to hear about the good time she had, even if she could remember it. And probably she couldn't, not after the rufy.

But, looking like she did, there was nothing here Files wanted from her. Not now. Banged up face, body all wrapped so you couldn't even tell she was a woman or not. All that time in the car driving up here, stupid waste of time, for nothing. Zip. Zilch.

He had to get out of this place, get back home to Vegas, back with the action. Just as soon as David worked out the thing with Wince.

"Okay then," he said. "You take it easy, okay?" He handed the cup back to Malcolm and left.

Everything was cool. Shirley never said word one, and Malcolm didn't know his hat from his ass. Nothing needed fixing. Files tugged the Glock out of his waistband and slid it under the driver's seat.

Pedal to the metal, like they say, and he flew down the interstate. The fuzz buster he'd picked up at the Gallup Kmart did the job. It beeped to signal the trap near a village called Thoreau. It beeped another time just past the Continental Divide marker. Each time it warned him maybe a mile out. The first trap he sailed past at 65 mph, peering straight ahead through the bug-smeared windshield and never saw the cops, wherever they were parked. The second one was only a couple minutes later, so soon it pissed him off enough that he slowed to 50 to look for them. He stuck a hand out the window to flip off the Firebird half-hidden beside the old Stuckey's on the hill.

Then he made up the time. With the setting sun behind him, the Caddy's shadow stretching out ahead longer and fainter like a guide in the fading light, he held 105 mph until he hit the windy curve east of Acoma. The Caddy fluttered left on its shocks and forced him to slow until it flattened out at the far end of the curve and he could punch it.

By the time he topped the last hill and saw the lights of Albuquerque backed against the Sandia Mountains, Files had decided how to wrap things up. If David didn't want to, Files would. He'd force Wince to sell the fuckin' restaurant. Take charge and get done with this shit. He was sick of baby-sitting David. He wanted to go home.

Wince loved shrimp. Lobster, not so much. Lobster tasted like whatever you dunked it in. Butter, or mayonnaise, tartar sauce, ketchup…they were the real flavor of lobster, to him. He didn't need to prove sophistication by raving over lobster. But shrimp had its own spice, and texture, and appeal—more like blue collar seafood. He watched Rolan and David demolishing their lobster and Leela pushing bits of chicken around her plate, while he took seconds on shrimp from the buffet serving line.

"You don't know what you're missing," Rolan said.

"What I know is, one of history's great unsung heroes is the first man ever to pick up a lobster and take a bite out of it. I know I couldn't do it. Look at that." He pointed at the remains of Rolan's lobster, scraps of claw and carapace split and fragmented on a spare plate. "That thing looks like a salt-water bug, the roach-of-the-sea."

"Uh-huh." Rolan examined the remaining shrimp in front of Wince. "While you eat pink commas."

"Not any more. I've had enough. … Leela?"

"Ready when you are." She looked a question at David.

"Look around. You see how much these people are enjoying themselves. That's part of why we're here. The rest is, I want to go through some numbers with you and Rolan. But first, Mr. Tedescu would like to say hello."

"Why?"

"He was my boss, here. *The Shangri-La* is his. I managed it for him. It's his airplane, his hotel.... We should say hello."

"And the problem with that man before? The security man...?" Leela asked.

Wince watched David mull over his answer.

When it came, it was perfunctory. "A misunderstanding," David said. "When I left the *Shangri-La*, several people were upset. But not Mr. Tedescu. And he'd be pleased if we could meet with him."

"The owner?" Rolan said. He nodded, a big smile in place. "Sure, if that's what he wants."

Wince said, "The golden rule at work."

"His office is upstairs, kind of the casino's control room. Won't take a minute."

Leela looked at her watch. "He's in his of fice, now? It's almost eight."

"His long hours are why *The Shangri-La* is successful."

"I'd like to meet him. He's part of the package," Rolan said.

Leela nodded and pushed back from the table "Let's go."

Wince followed her past people still working on their meals. Walking along with the others in his party, swerving to avoid the seated diners, Wince sorted though the others' reactions to the crowd.

David was ignoring them and pointed toward the exit and his boss' office somewhere upstairs.

Rolan looked side to side, scanning everything as if committing to memory the scene around them: a crowded restaurant, filled with the excited chatter of the sated diners.

Leela seemed to see nothing but David's back, as she pursued him, towed along by his determination.

Anticipating, Wince trailed them all.

David used his key to summon Mr. Tedescu's private elevator…and, using it, had to wonder why they'd forgotten to reclaim it from him when he left. It was a reminder of the day when this had been *his* private elevator, too, not only Mr. Tedescu's. The elevator doors were nearly concealed behind a pair of lush potted ficus, and the elevator led not to all the upper floors of *The Shangri-La* but only to the anteroom outside Mr. Tedescu's office.

The receptionist's desk wasn't manned when David led the others past it toward the double doors. Sheree had gone home for the day. Too bad. He would have enjoyed demanding the apology his return had earned. Well…another time.

The double doors stood ajar. David held up a hand to stop Wince and the Begays while he leaned into the doorway. "Mr. Tedescu?"

"Come in."

David led the way into *the presence*. The hunky was garbed entirely in light blue, again. He was seated on a raised platform. Ranked across from him were three canvas director's chairs, each labeled with a name across the back. "L.Begay, R.Begay, R.Wince." No chair for David. He bit his tongue and stayed mum.

"Welcome. Please take a seat," Mr. Tedescu said, pointing at the chairs. "Alphabetically. … Tee Jay, come join me." He indicated another director's chair beside him on the platform. "Up here." He beckoned, then said, "Thank you all for coming. I hope the trip was pleasant?" It wasn't rhetorical. He waited for someone to speak.

Before David could take over, Rolan said, "Very nice, thank you. And your casino's really impressive."

"Tee Jay wanted you to see how we do things here. *The Shangri-La's* not the biggest casino in Las Vegas, but it's the most successful…in the only way that matters. Tell him. Tee Jay. What's our Return On Investment this year."

David stood beside Tedescu and recited. "Twenty-three percent, R.O.I., up from twenty-two four last year." He turned to Mr. Tedescu,

"Right. Twenty-three frigging percent! We amortized initial costs in five years! We can probably even top that in your new casino, on the reservation. And that's the reason we'll be able pay your people ten percent…after we've recovered construction costs, of course."

David cringed. Too early in the argument! The old man was giving away one of the clinchers! David had planned the entire pitch, from enticement…to persuasion. And now Mr. Tedescu was screwing up the plan.

Rolan turned his smile to Leela. "You hear that? Ten percent!"

"I hear it. Will the council get to see that in writing?"

David's took a deep breath and flashed his best smile. "Absolutely! That's what I've been talking about. We can get together on this. Just give me the chance to work with the council. It won't take a long to firm up details." He looked at Mr. Tedescu, who nodded. "Right, then," David said. "Say, a month."

Rolan repeated the figure with awe. "Ten percent!"

Wince leaned back and stretched out his legs. "I'd probably ask...ten percent of what?" he said. "Ten percent...of their twenty-three percent Are Oh Eye? Or ten percent of whatever they *net*, after amortizing construction costs, and development." He looked at David.

David nodded. Damn! This gomer was sticking his nose in. Another breath. "Exactly!" he said. And then, "And contingencies, of course."

"Whoa!" Leela said, standing. "That's pretty much a one-way street, wouldn't you say?" She glared at Mr. Tedescu.

"Tee Jay can clarify it."

Great! Mr. Tedescu botched everything and left it for others to fix.

"I want to hear that," Rolan said.

"Tee Jay will explain." Mr. Tedescu stood. "Oh, and take the chairs with you. Just keep them, my gift. But before you go, let me ask Mr. Wince...why are you here?"

"Two-day vacation."

"Do I understand, you might advise your friends to help us with our plans?"

Wince laughed. "Oh, I don't think so. That's up to them."

"But you have been meeting with Mr. David, is that true?"

"Once or twice," David said. He had to head this off!

"He's met with me," Wince said. "I've never gone to see him, but he has visited a project I have underway."

Mr. Tedescu looked at David. "Why is that?"

David looked at Wince, shaking his head. "No reason. Just curiosity."

Mr. Tedescu nodded. "Well…." He stepped off the platform. "Enjoy the rest of your visit. We may be partners one day. I look forward to that. … Tee Jay?"

"Yes Sir?"

"Take them home. Come back when you have an agreement. One that benefits both you and me."

Jesus! How did he get that? Before David could answer, Wince's cell phone rang. Wince flipped it open and turned his back to them, hunched over the phone.

David couldn't hear. He watched Wince freeze, then straighten up, turn to face them, still concentrating on a voice on the phone.

Wince closed the phone and tucked it into a shirt pocket. He said, "How fast can we get back to Albuquerque?"

"What's wrong?" Leela asked.

Rolan said, "What's up, Man?"

"Elliott's in the hospital."

"Elliott? What—"

"And Buck says Sunrise Plaza caught fire. He's there right now. Watching it burn."

$ **27** $

Albuquerque drinks Colorado snow-pack. Winter's snow-fall accumulation begins to melt in late March and continues through summer till the first frost in late August, when temperatures along the Front Range dip again. Till then, melting snow trickles south, each seeping snowdrift loosing a rivulet. Those sparkling tiny ribbons merge as creeks, streams, then finally become the river that snakes its swelling way through Colorado. It grows till it earns its name, big river.

The *Río Grande* surges south through New Mexico and Texas, roiling mud-laden in deep canyons, diminished here and there as its volume seeps away to refill the shallow pocket aquifers below. *Asequias* and natural ditches of farmland dependant on the annual flow drain off even more. And Albuquerque, largest single drain on the river water, fills its reservoir near the fairgrounds while the river seeps into scores of underground aquifers in the Rio Grande valley. The reservoir feeds the city's lawn sprinklers, thirsty homeowners, car washes…and fire hoses.

That was the sequence Wince mentally rehearsed. Not to fuel any optimism. Only to fill his imagination and avoid picturing the annihilation of Sunrise Plaza. To block the dread he felt.

At 6:10 a.m. he boarded the earliest Southwest Airlines

flight out of McCarran International Airport and strapped into a third row aisle seat, tense and impatient for the flight to lift off and take him home. Once in the air, he pictured the rivers beneath the cloud cover moving south below him toward a single, specific reservoir…and water system…and city water mains…and canvas hoses…and fire. *The* fire. His construction site.

Concentrating on the sequence, he tried not to picture the damage awaiting him. He avoided imagining the only way he knew how. Concentrate on something else. Fill your mind with random scenes. Like biting the bullet so you don't feel the surgeon's knife. It worked… for minutes at a time.

In two hours he'd know whether he faced damage…or disaster.

He took a deep breath and surrendered to circumstance. Accept what you can't avoid, he told himself. Use it. The fire—no matter what had triggered it—represented a quick reshuffling of the deck. A handful of wild cards tossed into the larger game underway. He couldn't ignore the new circumstance. He really had no choice. He had to incorporate it among the problems he faced.

In fact, he hoped to find in it a solution to those problems. When life gives you lemons…and so on.

Twice he called Buck Tsosie to ask for details. No use. Buck's cell phone was turned off. Or the battery was dead.

Elliott didn't answer his cell, either. And the telephone receptionist at University Hospital wouldn't say anything about Chávez's condition.

She didn't even confirm that he'd been admitted.

And Wince couldn't think of anyone else to call.

Nothing to do but endure the flight, in ignorance. And hope.

David's eggs were runny and the bacon was half-raw. No way he'd let that pass, if he were still managing *Shangri-La*. But it wasn't his problem, now. He didn't care. If this was the worst that happened today...

He sat in a corner booth at *The Shangri-La* coffee shop and shoved his plate away. Almost 8:00 a.m. He'd tried talking Wince into staying but finally took the stubborn gomer to the airport and drove back to *The Shangri-La*, pissed off at the problem he saw developing. Wince was gone. Out of reach.

Nothing he could do about it, David had to focus on the meeting that Mr. Tedescu demanded. This afternoon. Upstairs in the small conference room. Between them, David hoped, he and Mr. Tedescu could sell the two Indians on the casino project in Window Rock. And that would content the hunky.

Okay, why not? If it didn't work, David had a back-up plan, a better way out of the mess Mr. Tedescu had him in.

The girl was the biggest problem, for now.

She'd wanted to fly with Wince back to Albuquerque, but her brother and Wince talked her out of it. Nothing she could do there. And Rolan persuaded her to stay to hear David's complete pitch, after lunch.

David knew he was ready, if Mr. Tedescu didn't interfere. Something was going on there. The hunky bastard was a generation past it now, too old and out of touch, but he still had a nose for details. He'd picked up hints somewhere in the past week and was paying more attention to Wince than David liked.

It made sense that Wince wouldn't hang around to beg a ride back to Albuquerque, later, when the Indians went. He was all hot to check out the damage to his little motel remodel, the low-rent instant slum he was building. But David couldn't send the hunky's jet back to Albuquerque just to accommodate Wince. Mr. Tedescu would scotch that. So...a compromise. David bought Wince a ticket on the earliest Southwest flight back, bought it out of his own pocket, and even drove Wince to McCarran.

He drained his coffee cup and checked his watch again. 8:10. Almost time to round up the Indians and walk them through the smaller casinos off the strip and down on Freemont Street. A tour, show them what a boutique casino could look like. Then lunch, and hit them with the Power Point presentation he'd worked up. By 2:30 or 3:00 he'd know whether they'd help make the Window Rock casino a go.

Not that it mattered all that much. Plan B was his real out, and it was riding with Wince, already somewhere south of Lake Mead.

From the Sunport to Lomas Avenue, even on side streets, was only a ten-minute sprint. But passing the last car lot on Lomas, Wince backed off and let his Mustang coast the final block. No fire engines in sight. No firefighters, or barricades, or canvas hoses. From where he sat, it all looked like a non-event.

Until he parked outside Sunrise Plaza, opened the car door and stepped into the musty breeze.

Smoke on the wind.

It wasn't wood smoke. The scent of wood smoke is domestic and inviting, not like this. The stench in the air told its own story. The stink of electrical fire, burnt rubber, something sour, and wrong.

Then Wince saw the gate in the temporary site fence, twisted off its hinges and hanging ajar. The gap wore two strips of yellow crime-scene tape, and a printed notice. He didn't read it. He snatched it off the fence, pulled loose the yellow tape, and went inside, through the office, into the courtyard. The stench was stronger here in the hazy air. Like burnt feathers.

"Hey!" A stranger in some kind of uniform accosted him. "What the hell? Didn't you read the sign?"

"This one?" Wince held out the crumpled notice in his hand. "I guessed what it said." He tossed it to the man.

His clothes were gray denim, almost a leisure suit, not any working uniform Wince could recognize. Not fireman's garb. Not police blues.

"This is a closed site," the man said. He folded his arms, blocking Wince's path. He was squat, in his fifties and—his pose said—in charge. "Wait out front, and I'll—"

"No." Wince brushed past him.

"Back off, I said!" He grabbed Wince's arm. "Wait out front."

"It's my place." Wince stared the man's grip off his sleeve. "I need to know what—"

"And I need to see some I.D. Until I do, it's *my* place, not yours. I.D., now...or drag your ass out of here." The man leaned forward, waiting, up on his toes.

"You want to try to 'drag' me?"

"Relax, *primo*. Just come up with some I.D."

Wince flipped open his wallet to show his driver's license. "Robert Wince. I own the place."

"That's what I heard. You and your partner, like the names on the sign out front. The rescue squad took Chávez to the hospital, last night. University Hospital, I think." He flashed a badge and his own identification. "Cruz Romero. AFD arson." He tucked the wallet into a hip pocket of his denims. "Looks like that's what we got here."

"Arson?"

"Pretty clear. Let me show you." Romero led the way up the courtyard staircase toward the back of the building. "*Mira.* Look, don't touch. Just keep your hands in your pocket." He pointed past a ribbon of yellow crime-scene tape strung across the doorway of number 4.

The apartment's gaping, glassless windows stared at them like black-rimmed, vacant eyes. Here the acrid stench was even stronger. The balcony walkway fronting the second-floor units was littered with broken glass, a slashed window frame and shingle-sized patches of broken drywall and slivered pine. Water stains marked the floor. The strips of splintered wallboard that had survived the firemen's axes stood like so many fiberboard stalagmites, a ragged fence.

Wince kicked his way through the glass shards rattling like gravel underfoot and leaned over the railing to look. He spotted more water stains tracing their way down the walls below. The courtyard was cluttered with debris tossed off the second level to float in the puddles left by the fire hoses.

"Hey! Watch it. Back off there!"

Wince whirled to face him and took a deep breath.

Romero held up both hands, fending off any comments Wince had. "I know, man. I know. It's a bitch."

"You said 'arson'?"

"We don't know who, but 'how' is real clear. We've got a lot to go on." He beckoned and pointed through the doorway. "It started at the baseboard in the back corner there and spread down this way. The Tyvek insulation retarded the spread up the wall, and your sprinkler system damped it some, but it didn't douse it. Not enough volume from your emitters there. You better check them." He pointed toward the ceiling inside the apartment. "But they kept the spread down till we could get hoses in here. Pretty lucky we got here fast, if you want to know."

"Yeah. *Lucky.*"

"No, it was. Your guy Chávez called 911, and for once they responded quick. Another couple minutes, the whole place might have gone up."

"That's the lucky part?" Wince shook his head.

"I know. That's not how you feel right now, but take a minute to think it over You've got all the stink you could want, but the stink will fade. I'd guess only this unit, maybe the one below, really got fucked up."

"Yes, they did that."

Romero nodded. "All right, these two will need a lot of work. About the rest"—his waving hands indicated the other units—"about them, you decide."

"Arson, you said. Walk me through it."

"The accelerant was gasoline. We found two empty Dasani bottles inside there. They stunk from the gasoline the doer brought in. He poured gas along the wall, then tossed the bottles. One melted down, but the other was laying outside the flames. It's pretty much intact."

"Any fingerprints?"

"After a fire? Probably not. We're not C.S.I., that high-tech Sherlock Holmes baloney they do on the Tee Vee. Those C.S.I. guys can find latent prints on somebody's breath."

"What the hell kind of bottles—"

"Calm down, now. I tagged them and sent them back in the evidence bag. We got the bottles, a twist of burlap still stinking with gas, and we took up samples from the worst burned spot on the floor. More than enough to prove arson. We'll sort this out fast. For now, it's enough we know.

"What we *don't* know is, was it kids playing in here? They do that, you know. Find an empty building to sit in and drink themselves shit-faced. And maybe start a fire, it gets out of hand..."

Wince looked at him. "That's what you really think?"

"Hell no! It was intentional, is what I think.

Somebody came in all prepped, equipped, soaked a spot on the floor and set it off with burlap fuse. But thinking it"—he held out a hand, palm up—"and proving it"—he opened the other hand—"are pretty far apart, for now. So that's my job. Closing that gap." He brought his palms together and squeezed nothing.

Wince shook his head, then shrugged. He handed Romero his card. "Call me and tell me what you find out. Anything at all."

Romero pointed into the courtyard. "Let's go down there and talk about it. Somebody said you were out of town."

The tone of voice stopped Wince. He peered at Romero. "You mean, do I have an alibi?"

"Back off, *primo*. All I mean is. were you out of town? Simple question."

"You think I'd torch my own place?"

"It's happened."

"Get the hell out of here!" Wince pushed past him.

"Hey! I got more questions."

Wince waved him away and walked out.

$ **28** $

"**How's your head?**" Wince stood in the doorway and smiled at Chávez in his hospital bed.

"Sore, what do you think?"

"They wouldn't let me come in till after lunch. You doing okay?"

"Little dizzy, not much. They tell you when they're letting me out of here?" He lay propped on a pair of folded pillows. A bald patch above his left ear revealed a row of stitches under the iodine, or mercurochrome, or merthiolate, or whatever the orange stain was. The patch was ugly, but not swollen.

Wince pointed at the other bed in the room, empty now. "Long as you've got a private room, you ought to rest. They'll let you out when you won't fall on your face."

"Hey, I'm good as ever." Chávez swung his legs over the side of the bed and moved to stand up but didn't make it. He sagged back against the pillows. "*Whooo*, shit!" he said. "Room's spinning. Like I'm drunk."

"Take it easy." Wince put a firm hand on Chávez's shoulder. "Don't hurry everything here. What do the doctors say?"

"Maybe a concussion. No fracture, mostly headache, but it's clearing up. ... They tell you what happened?"

"Not yet. What do you know?"

"I went out there to get my T-square." He answered

Wince's questioning look. "I was gonna frame a couple pictures I took of the site. You know—before and after views of Sunrise Plaza. When we're rich and famous we can show people our humble start.

"So I was digging in my tool chest when I saw a light up in number four. Didn't hear anything, just a light moving around. Like a flashlight. So I went up to check. Before I got there I smelled gasoline and saw this, like...like a flare going off. Not a big explosion, y'know?. A little *poof*, and then...the fire. I punched in 911 on my cell and told them the address while I ran. The guy who hit me was behind the door. I never got a look at him. I go in through the door and the fucker whacks me in the head. Here." Chávez touched the wound. And flinched.

"You said 'he.' You sure?"

"What? You mean, was it a woman? Man, he really whacked me! Maybe Holly Holm could hit that hard, but not your average *chica*. The asshole who clocked me didn't hold back. *Wham!* Like to tear my head off."

"You think Stapely'd do it?"

"He doesn't have the balls for it."

"Then, who?"

"You tell me."

Wince shrugged in resignation. "The cops will find him. Or the AFD arson squad."

"You believe that?"

"Let it go. More important for us, what happens now?"

"New ballgame. We've got this to deal with." Wince held up his cell phone and showed Chavez the display screen. "The fire was only last night. I don't know how much damage was done, how long it'll delay us, whether the buyers Quintana had lined up are still committed…and what's here?" He tapped the screen. "Twelve messages, already."

"They moved faster than the fire department. Who called?'

"Mostly creditors. A couple of numbers I don't know. What I do know is, they're piling up on us, and the ashes haven't cooled yet."

"So…we're fucked," Chávez slumped back against the pillows.

"Not yet."

"How can you—"

"Not if we work this right. It's another complication, that's all. I'll take care of it."

Wince looked out the window at the churn of traffic on the street below. He thought a moment before saying, "How'd you like to change our letterhead?"

"Say what?"

"I've been thinking.

"Usually one of the problems," Chávez said.

Wince wrote a phrase on the air with one sweeping hand. "Chávez. Construction," he said. "After we finish Sunrise, I'm turning everything over to you. You're earned it, and I'll be busy working on my cabin. The company's yours."

"What are you talking about?"

"It ought to be 'Chavez Construction,' anyway."

"Yeah, yeah, that's cool. But what I mean is…what cabin?"

"The place down at Elephant Butte."

"What? That shell you showed me? There's no roof on the place!"

"Right, but it stands in the middle of six big cottonwoods,

three acres on the mesa east of the lake. There's the house and barn..." He found himself picturing the property.

"Gonna take a lot of work."

"That's the best part of it. ...I started roughing out a schedule."

"You bought it? Bought it with what?"

"Promises, like always. I was going to tell you."

"Jesus, Robert! It's one more thing to worry about."

"No sweat. My point is, things aren't that bad. I like planning. You like doing. We'll finish Sunrise, then I'll plan, and you'll...heal."

Chávez nodded. "So you think the future's looking good."

Wince said, "Let me handle these phone calls, then I'll be back and we'll talk."

"Does that mean I get custody of Stapely."

"That was my hope. —For now, you rest."

"Are we changing the name? 'Chávez Construction?' My mother'll like that."

"Tell her, if you want. The doctors will probably send you home tomorrow. You and I will talk...when one of us is thinking straight."

"¿Qué pasa, Tomás?" Eloy Sanchez slid his chair back from the desk, put his hands behind his head and stretched broadly. He leaned forward to close the account book he was working on. "Two minutes. I've got to finish this." He indicated a sheaf of forms on his desktop.

"I knew you'd want to hear right away," Jones said. "We got him! Wince. He's totally screwed. There was a fire at his building project last night, and everything's going to hit the fan for him. Watch everybody foreclose on him."

"Really?"

"He can't sell a place that's burned down, and he owes everybody. Suppliers. His crew. The bank. Nothing he can—"

"Burned down? That's not what I hear."

"Well, okay, maybe not all the way. But damaged, for sure."

"How did this fire happen? It was kind of convenient, ¿qué no?"

"Oh, I don't know about that," Jones said. But I know you bought a shit-load of his debts."

"So now I call the notes, and wait forever to collect. Or foreclose, if I want to own a burnt-out motel."

"I just know he's got to pay the people he owes. And the only way Wince can pay you...he's got to sell *Half-Off.*" His smile was smug. "He's got nothing else."

Sanchez sighed. "So he sells that *pinche* restaurant of his. He sells that, then he pays me what he owes. Is that it?"

"How much is that?"

Sanchez cocked his head and smiled. It's what my bean-counters call 'confidential,' okay?"

"Sorry, Eloy. Of course. That's between you and...them, the bean-counters. "He shook his head as if clearing it. "But how—"

"Maybe I'll buy the restaurant myself, 'between me and Wince. Directly. Skip any middle man, or broker, or agent, you know? 'cause what if Wince sells it to someone else, while you're diddling around with it.? Why don't I do it that way?"

"C'mon, Eloy. I got this all set up." Jones seized a chair and slid it in front of Sanchez's desk. He dropped into the chair and began to talk. He started in logic, and argument, and shifted to pleading. He dragged in Sanchez's daughters and the pride they would feel when he was able to get them the restaurant they wanted to own. He even tried confessing to setting the fire, the only way he'd seen to get Wince off the dime, he said, but Sanchez laughed off the confession.

Jones resorted to begging for understanding, and forgiveness, and support...and was saved by the boredom he saw dimming Sanchez's eyes.

"Enough!" Sanchez said. "Do it, don't come back till he agrees. I wanted a signed bill of sale, title insurance, the works. In one week.. Six hundred kay, no more."

"*A week?* Jeez, Eloy, I don't know if..." He flinched at Sanchez look. "Okay, sure, I can do it. One week. You got it!"

Sanchez went back to his paperwork.

El Gato Negro was near enough the Hilton that Files could walk to it. He'd seen the bar's flickering neon sign out his hotel room window minutes after David checked him in, and he'd stopped by twice in the past few days for a couple of drafts. Not really good beer, but better than the Mexican-labelled panther piss the regulars in *The Black Cat* were drinking. And there was a pool table in the back where Files won twenty bucks from a couple of greasers who didn't know shit about nine-ball. It gave him something to do while he waited for Malcolm Obee.

Obee was already on the road when he phoned. Some crap about Shirley remembered or found out it was Files she had a drink with—only she told her husband it was only soda pop—the night she got bumped around and bruised a little. So Obee wanted details or confessions or recollections or whatever Files could come up with. And nothing would discourage him taking the three-hour drive from his Indian village down to quiz Files.

Obee walked in out of the afternoon sunshine at 3:00, squinting to find Files in the dark bar. "Ahh, there you are," he said, offering Files a half-wave.

"Back in a minute," Files told Pedro or José or whatever-the-hell his name was. "Rack 'em up. And this time gimme a tight rack."

He waved for Obee to follow him out the back door into the alley.

"You need to tell me what went on with you and Shirley last week," Obee said. "She doesn't remember it all but she—"

Files swung once and broke Obee's jaw. The second punch knocked the man up against the brick wall of the building where he slid to the ground, unconscious. It also hurt Files's hand. *Damn it!* He dropped the cue ball he carried.

He felt the bruised knuckles with his other hand and found nothing broken. He sucked at two fingers but they still hurt. "Shit!" he said. He kicked Obee twice in the ribs and swaggered back into the bar. Where he won another $32 before he returned to the Hilton.

$ 29 $

By the time Wince was able to attack the list of phone messages demanding attention, the dozen waiting for him had become 16. Three were calls from his crew. Of the three, only Whistler offered his sympathy. The other two wanted to know when—or whether— they could come back to work. Stapely called to say, "You had it coming, you sonovabitch! You ever get your car fixed?" He hung up laughing.

Tom Jones demanded a meeting. It was urgent, he said. In fact, he announced that he was coming by at 9:00 a.m. "to settle everything."

T.J. David asked to see him about 10:00 and left a phone number.

Eight of the other calls were from creditors. Five accepted Wince's assurance that the fire would cause only a temporary delay. One said he'd turned his account over to a collector. Two said they'd sold the debt. Wince promised them all that their bills would be paid. He smiled when he spoke to warm his voice. He asked for patience.

The call he'd been expecting came from the Zia State Bank. A voice on the tape informed Wince that his construction loan had been sold ("reassigned," the speaker said, chuckling at the euphemism). It was now held by Sanchez Family Finance. And Sanchez would expect "prompt resolution of the debt."

Wince thumbed the phone silent and smiled. He clicked his tongue, counting. It was like hearing the next tumbler fall in a combination lock.

Tsosie's gift shop. Click.

Sanchez's debt acquisition. Click.

David's upcoming appointment. Click.

Wince was still smiling when the knock came at the door.

Wince opened it, ands sagged. He nodded a tired greeting and leaned against the doorframe. "I knew I should install a peephole," he said. "I keep putting it off."

"You're too busy, is what I hear," Dan Chutters said. "You got a minute?" He entered and closed the door behind him "I was on my way home and decided to stop."

"You live near here?"

"South Valley, down toward Isleta."

"Uh-huh. So how am I on your way home?"

"I thought you wouldn't want to come downtown. I waited till I was off the clock and came to save you that trip."

"This is unofficial?" At Chutters' nod, Wince said, "I'll get you a beer."

"Skip it. Let's talk about your new friends. Did you get my message from Chávez?"

"I got it."

"And...?"

"The Vegas guys you're worried about aren't in town to see me. They came to talk to Rolan."

"Isn't that like talking to you? Rolan Begay, your partner."

"Not partners, this time. Just friends."

Chutters looked around and spotted a wooden captain's chair. He pointed at it, raising an eyebrow,

"Go ahead." Wince watched the man settle in. It was starting to look like a long conversation. He decided not to help it along. He paced in front of Chutters, no intent of sitting. If he hoped to embarrass the man out of his chair, and out of the house…no luck.

"I went by your new place," Chutters said. "Sunrise Plaza?"

"Pretty much of a mess," Wince said. "You want to tell me *why* you went by?"

Chutters' expression said that ought to be obvious. "I talked with Romero, the AFD investigator. He says 'arson.' He told you about it."

"He told me. And he's the one investigating. So what's your interest?"

"Romero will try to I.D. whoever set the fire. If it's a familiar M.O., he'll get the guy. He's pretty good. But you could help. First, what's changed for you in the past few days, or weeks?"

"I don't get you."

"Any new enemies you didn't know about? Anyone pissed at you?"

"Of course. Every day. Buyers, if I don't get their apartment ready in time. Creditors who have their own bills to pay. Guys on my crew, if I chew them out for screwing up the job."

"Anyone special? Because that's who Romero will be looking for."

Wince ran through a mental list, then shook his head. "A couple of *bobos* say they hate me, but Elliott can't believe they've got the balls to act on it."

"Give me the names."

"No. I'm not messing up somebody innocent."

"*Innocent?* Maybe the innocents you won't name, they'd surprise you."

"However it shakes out, when Romero I.D.s this enemy of mine…*if* he does, then what?"

"The case gets handed over to APD. Arson is a crime, maybe you heard."

"Yeah, I've heard." There didn't seem to be a way to cut Chutters off. Best to let him have his say. "So you get to arrest the villain, is that it? You, personally?"

"Not usually, but if the doer is anybody off your crew, or anybody might be a friend of yours. Or a friend of Chávez's. And if there's an insurance payoff comes out of it, then it gets to be my problem. The fire itself doesn't interest me all that much. Fraud does."

"Oh, that clears it up. I got it. If I'm screwed, APD might try to find the arsonist. But if I come out of this mess even, if the insurance policy covers our loss, then Elliott and I will have cops all over us. Especially you."

Chutters nodded. "Especially me."

"Well, that's not going to happen. So forget it." Wince waved his thumb toward the door.

Chutters folded his arms and settled deeper into his chair. "Maybe you can tell me about David and Files." He offered a self-satisfied smile. "Yeah, I know their names."

"Why? You think they set the fire?"

"That's a different issue. But you can tell me what the two of them want in Albuquerque."

"Hey, c'mon, Chutters! Why—"

"It's 'Dan,' okay?"

"Okay, Dan. —Why don't you go ask them? It's not like they report to me."

"We both know they're here to see you. They been hanging around your dad's restaurant and over at Sunrise, both. You took them up the tram—"

"I didn't 'take' them. I had business at the crest. They followed. For all I know, they went for the tram-ride, like any other tourist."

Chutters stretched his legs. "Okay. You're going to make me pull teeth, is that the way it goes?" He rose to stand face-to-face with Wince. "What do you know about them?"

"Probably less than you do, from the sound of it. They're looking to open a gift shop, is what they said."

"Uh-huh. Selling flowers and teddy bears? Not likely.— They're trouble. Especially Files."

Wince shrugged. "It's not my business."

"Did you know that Files has been inside?"

"So have I."

Chutters smiled as if he'd just won a bet. "I was going to get to that."

"There's no connection. I did less than a deuce in Santa Fe. Files probably never saw the place. We were in different lockups, at different times. I never met the guy till he showed up at *Half-Off*. Even then, I talked mainly to the one called David. He's meeting with Rolan, trying to learn about gift shops for a casino he wants to run. The other one... Files? He's David's go-fer, drives his car, carries his bags."

"Do you know where they are now?"

"How would I know? Probably back in Las Vegas."

Chutters pounced. "Yeah, where *you* were this weekend."

"Uh-huh. Where I was this weekend...when somebody else torched Sunrise. You got that? I was out of town, when the fire happened. Does that clear me?"

"Why were you in Las Vegas?"

"Why's anybody go to Vegas? I went to see a couple of shows. The Blue Man Group, or a strip show with naked girls riding naked ponies, really artistic." Wince opened the door and stood waiting. "So now...how about you saddle up your pony and ride on home?"

Smile gone, Chutters said, "You're a tough man to help."

"People who want help ask for it."

Chutters pried himself out of the chair, reluctant. "Okay, have it your way. But I get the feeling we'll see each other again."

"Good with me. —Bring me the guy who torched my place, I'll be happy to see you."

"You have a good night." Chutters walked out, tossing a final shot over his shoulder. "Be careful playing with matches."

Wince closed the door. That went well, he thought, checking his watch. Almost 9:00. Time for the Fox early newscast. He hit the speed dial on his cell and called Dion's to order a pizza.

$ 30 $

"You disappoint me, Artie," Mr. Tedescu said. "I asked you to monitor Tee Jay's activities. Do you recall that?"

"Sure." Files felt like a fool, standing in this crummy motel room with his pants bunched down around his ankles. Talking to a man who wasn't even in the room. The phone-call caught him at the wrong time. Ten seconds earlier, he'd been too busy to answer the fuckin' phone. Right in the middle of the short strokes Now he stood with his back to the bed. He couldn't see Jasmine, or Yasmine, or whatever, but he felt her checking out his bare legs. He clenched his toes to knot up the calf and bunch the muscle. "Sure, I remember."

"Do you have any more to say?"

"Uh…I remember *good*?"

"No Artie. Do you have any more to say in regard to Tee Jay? What's he up to? He's spending all his time in Albuquerque. Why's he not in Window Rock?"

"Uhh, Mr. Tedescu, I think he's working on the Wince guy. I been hanging around, watching. It's Wince and—"

"Yes, Artie, I know that. I met Wince when he and the two Indians were here. So you believe David is playing him. Is that it?"

Files heard a noise and turned to look.

Jasmine lay stretched out on her stomach. She slipped off the bed like she was a snake coming toward him. Hands

210

reaching over the edge of the bed, then elbows, she slithered to the floor. She squirmed around some, gave him a big phony smile, and beckoned him with both hands. "Come get thome more," she whispered. "We ain't done, Thweetie."

Mr. Tedescu said something in the phone that Files didn't hear.

Files motioned for the girl to be quiet and hold still. He was having trouble answering Mr. Tedescu and watching Jasmine at the same time.

"Say that again?"

"Am I interrupting something important?"

"What?"

Mr. Tedescu got so quiet he might have been whispering, too. "Stop whatever you're doing and listen to me."

"Yes Sir, Mr. Tedescu. I'm listening." Files tried walking over to the bed to sit down, but his pants were tangled around his ankles and he staggered. He hopped in clumsy lunges and motioned Jasmine to shut up. "But maybe we got a bad connection."

"What does he want from Wince?"

"I don't know that, sir. But I think we got Wince's attention, finally."

"Maybe you could ask Tee Jay. And call me back with the information. Does that sound like something you might do?"

Jasmine was kneeling beside him now, running her warm hands up his leg.

He slammed her with an elbow and turned away. "Damn it!" He flinched at the electric shock stinging him. He'd cracked his crazy bone.

"What was that?" Mr. Tedescu said. At least he was talking louder now.

"Nothing! Was really nothing. I bumped my fuckin' arm."

There was a pause. "I'm sorry to hear that. I hope your injury will heal. Now go locate Tee Jay. Tell him I'm not pleased and I expect him to phone me. At once! On the direct line."

"Yes Sir, I'll tell…" The phone was dead. Useless piece of crap!

He whacked Jasmine in the mouth with it.

Wrong! Now he had blood on his phone. He wiped it on his sleeve.

"Basthird!" She swatted at him but missed.

He hit her again, twice, and hopped away, pulling up his pants. He was done here. He hadn't planned to pay her anyway. Maybe he'd come back later, after he got David to focus for a change.

It was damn well David's turn! Files had worked it so they could go home, if David did his part!

Jasmine was still screaming at him when he left. And spitting! Rude bitch.

It took David three hours to find Tsosie's apartment. It wasn't in Albuquerque.

Using his laptop, David googled Tsosie's name and found him in the BIA registry of New Mexico Navajos, listed in the midst of at least one hundred Tsosies. He was "Leonard Buck Tsosie." The phone book gave David an address across the Rio Grande in a low-rise suburb called Rio Rancho.

David renamed it 'Dirtville.' Gusting winds swept dust

off the grassless housing projects and geometric grid of dirt roads. Yellow clouds drifted across the cab windshield, poked through invisible cracks in the door and window seals. The grit dusted David's pursed lips and settled between clenched teeth. He sat chewing and spat on the cab floor. How could anyone, even an Indian, live in this place?

David spent most of an hour sitting in the grimy cab with the meter ticking, waiting for Tsosie to show up. Since getting back from Vegas, he hadn't seen Files. No loss. Files had turned out to be less his driver and bodyguard than a spy for Mr. Tedescu. No reason to let Files, or anyone else, know he was talking to Tsosie.

Waiting let David revise the 'Wince-sheet' on his notepad. Two or three more questions to be answered, starting with Tsosie. Get the right answers, and he could tell all the Vegas losers who'd been on his case to shove it. He had a future without them. All it took was getting over on a couple of Beanerville's best. No sweat.

The cabbie turned to talk over his shoulder. "Hey Bro." He laid a hand on the ticking dash-mounted meter. "It's adding up. How long we going to sit here?"

"Till I say we leave." He pulled a fifty from the money clip he drew out of his blazer pocket and passed it forward. "How about you shut up till this is spent."

"You're the boss." The cabbie tucked the fifty into his shirt pocket.

"Yes I am."

They both leaned back to wait.

In twenty minutes, Tsosie pulled up and parked at the curb in a Ford 150 pick-up. He took two Furrs paper sacks out of the truck bed and carried them down a narrow sidewalk between a pair of garages.

"Wait here." David got out of the cab and followed.

He caught up with Tsosie at a two-story building behind the garages.

Tsosie was trying to unlock the door without putting down the bags he carried. Or spilling them.

"Let me do that for you," David said.

"Who are…? Oh, okay." He squirmed a quarter-turn and let David take the door key out of his hand while he braced his shopping bags against the doorframe.

David unlocked the door, took one of the shopping bags from Tsosie, and followed him into an empty room. He looked around for a table, a chair, somewhere to put the bag, but saw not a stick of furniture. A modular kitchen unit—stovetop, microwave, waist-high refrigerator—filled one wall. An open door across from it showed a small bathroom.

He followed Tsosie into the next room where four folding card table chair were ranked against one wall across from an army cot, covered by a tangled sheet and blanket.

"Anywhere," Tsosie said. He put his shopping bag on one of the chairs and sat down on another.

David took the cot. He tapped the bag beside him. "Groceries?"

"Some people think so." Tsosie reached into his bag and drew out a foot-high potted cactus. "You can make jelly, *pulque*, candy, ointment for burns and blisters…lots of uses for cactus. Rabbits eat them for the water. Cattle will, in bad years. Some people too. I'd rather have an apple, myself. But you can try one." He drew out another potted cactus and put it on the floor. "There's two more in your sack. I was planning to plant them. There, in the window box." He pointed at the window overlooking the alley. "I get tired looking out at pavement. My uncle used to say, once you make a parking lot, nothing ever grows there again but oil stains."

David shook his head. "I had a potted cactus once. It rotted. Nobody could tell me how much to water it."

"You ought to think about watering cactus once a month… but don't. Just think about it."

David stared his disbelief.

"The secret is, watch the weather report in the paper, and if you really got to water it, give it a spoonful every time it rains…in Yuma. That'll work." Tsosie reached under his cot and pulled out a six-pack of Dr. Pepper. "Want one?"

"You live here?" He couldn't imagine it. No closet, no place to hang your clothes. In fact, no clothes. None he could see.

Tsosie shook his head. "Gallup. I stay here if I have to come to the city. Not often."

"You know why I stopped by?"

"Sure. I've got something you want, and you're going to tell me why I should give it to you."

"No, I need to ask you something. If Wince sold his share of *Half-Off*, would you want to keep your half? Run the gift shop on your own? With a new partner?"

Tsosie looked at him and smiled. "You know, don't you, that 'my share' is a joke? It's only my name on the window."

"How'd it be if your share was real? Fifty-one per cent. In writing. A legal partnership."

Tsosie popped open the can of Dr. Pepper he held and drank.

David knew it was more delaying tactic than thirst. Looking for an answer, he watched Tsosie's eyes.

"Maybe I ought to talk to Quintana," Tsosie said. "He's a lawyer. He knows all about contracts."

"Quintana may know New Mexico law, I'll give him that. But you'd probably want to consult someone less…'local.'"

"I'd probably still like to check with an attorney."

"Buck, *I'm* an attorney. I wouldn't propose an arrangement that can't hold up in a court of law."

"So it would be totally legal." Tsosie asked.

"Or…unassailable."

Tsosie considered for a long moment before saying, "Robert thinks I could handle the gift shop. With him there, I could. Without him, I don't know. — Rolan, now. He'd be your man. He's got the experience and all. But him and me are two different people."

"If Wince stays, so will you. Is that right?"

"Can't tell," Tsosie said. "I only know I wouldn't do anything Robert didn't clear ahead of time."

"I can respect that. But let's assume that Wince likes the idea. And suppose you received…let's say, 'extra remuneration' for your agreement. It's a paper agreement, naming you fifty-one per cent owner. Just your name."

"What's the advantage?"

David couldn't believe it. How could he not know? "For you?"

"Advantages for *you*. You're the one making the offer."

David thought a moment. "Well, let's say Wince was right. Given the market, it's probably best to have a native Indian—isn't that what they say?—a native Indian selling Indian souvenirs. But remember, staff can be hired to do the grunt work. And for your cooperation, you'd receive, say, ten thousand dollars. One time payment. How does that sound?"

Tsosie took on a stern look. "Mr. David, that sounds a good bit like a bribe of some kind, or an attempt to—"

"Twenty."

"Well, that sounds less a bribe, more like a business proposition." Tsosie drew out another Dr. Pepper from beneath the cot and tossed it to David. "So now we're past the 'once upon a time' part. How about fleshing out the story? There's got to be more to it than I understand, so far."

David popped open the Dr. Pepper and raised it. A gesture. He didn't have to drink it. They got down to work.

$ **31** $

Jones arrived early. Wince had expected it and got to *Dim-mie's Half-Off* even earlier. He parked a block away, where the frontage road pulls off I-25, and sat trying to measure Jones's eagerness. Eager or not, Jones didn't have pockets deep enough to buy *Half Off*. But Wince decided to give him a chance to make his pitch.

Not because he liked Jones. He didn't. But because he did understand him. Jones worked for a cabal whose members felt superior because they'd chosen their parents better than Jones had. He kept his lobbyist's job by denying half his heritage. His *chicana* mother was acceptable enough to his employers. In fact, a plus. But an Anglo father—or at least the Anglo name—made him "coyote" to the Hispanos he worked for. It didn't matter much that most of them spoke even less Spanglish than he did. But they'd been U.S. tax-payers (or tax-avoiders) for four or five generations. And they had access to programs not open to someone named "Jones." It was a simple fact. His employers could cash in on their vic-tim-hood, based on the spelling of their family name.

The sad part was, Jones bought into it. He worked to help them profit from their surnames. It was nonsense, but Wince understood the power of the definition. He knew that being excluded from those feeding at the federal trough nagged at Jones. He felt like an outsider. Like Buck being a "church-builder" instead of "tobacco-people." Or Leela being a Begay miles away from Window Rock. Or being a Wince, anywhere.

So Wince sat parked a block away from the restaurant and watched Jones fidgeting in his car, hoping for a future what was improbable.

Tsosie arrived in his pickup, followed a scant three minutes later by Quintana, an attaché case swinging from one hand. Jones climbed from his car and hurried after them, almost running. Wince followed.

Quintana greeted him. "How's Elliott doing?"

"Getting better. He's griping about the food, and the lousy tee-vee reception in the hospital, with all the electronics gear they got there."

"Is he getting out soon?"

"I think so. I stopped by this morning and he was sitting on the edge of the bed, already dressed. He had to wait for the doctor."

"You think he was ready?" Quintana said.

"And eager. His head was already out of there. He was putting a move on the nurse."

"They let you see him that early?" Tsosie said. "I called the switchboard over there and they said no visitors till afternoon, unless you're family."

"I lied," Wince said. He glanced at Jones, standing near the serving counter, and nodded. "Nine o'clock, as promised. You want to get to it?"

Jones tried a weak smile. "I'm sorry about Chávez," he said. "I heard he got knocked cold, over at the fire. You tell him I asked about him, okay?"

"I'll do that. — Have you started without me?" He looked from Quintana to Jones.

Jones shook his head. "I brought you our offer, in writing." He held out a manila envelope.

But Wince waved it off. "Before we do that, I need to know why you want the place."

Bewildered, Jones said, "What do you mean, why do we want it? How long have I been talking to you about this? Now, before it's too late, we're gonna save the restaurant, before you screw it up with all this remodeling thing you started here." He frowned and waved at the mess around them. "We tried talking to Dimmie, your dad, about selling. Only he was always too stubborn even to talk."

"It was his—"

"I know, I know!" Jones changed his tack. "His restaurant, he could do what he wanted. But now he's gone, what's he care? So probably it's the right time for you to think about selling. Finally. And we want to run it just the way it is. Or *was*. The way it was before your guys started ripping and tearing in here."

Wince turned to Quintana. "You think this is ripping and tearing?"

Quintana shrugged. "I'd be more interested in what's in the numbers." He indicated the envelope Jones held.

"Not yet," Wince said. He pointed toward the adjoining room. "What's your plan for the big space back there?"

"What? The banquet room? Well…wedding receptions, Chamber of Commerce meetings, like that. Maybe rent it out for dances, after we improve the sound system. You've got the speakers positioned all wrong. There's feedback—"

"Okay, let that go. You don't mean storage."

"Storage won't generate a dime. And empty rooms don't produce income. You got to use the place better, Wince. Dimmie knew that, but you've been missing out on real opportunities. Counting income per square foot, *Half-Off*'s been a loser since you took over. I can get it back on its feet."

Quintana shook his head. "Hey, HO-nace. Hellova negotiating tactic. You want something from a guy, you start out insulting him and telling him he's doing a lousy job?"

"No, he's right," Wince said. He turned to Jones. "How about walking me through what you've got in mind?"

The verbal tour took a few minutes. Wince let Jones lead him through a description of what *Half-Off* could look like, under the 'right' management. Tsosie followed them, offering a running commentary on the tour. Wince listened. And Quintana sat on a stool, toying with a pair of bison-shaped ashtrays.

The conversation minutes made Wince reconsider Jones. The man had some good ideas for *Half-Off*. No telling if he could put them into practice, but he did make sense.

At the end of the tour, Wince accepted the envelope Jones clutched in his sweating hand. "What's it say?"

Jones looked at him. "It's our best offer. I worked Sanchez and the others to get that." He pointed at the envelope. "It's really the best offer you're gonna get. You'll take it, if you're smart."

Wince opened the envelope, read the slip of paper inside, but said nothing. He passed it to Tsosie. Quintana leaned close to read over Tsosie's shoulder. Jones stood waiting.

"I'll let you know," Wince said.

Jones flinched. "What's that mean, you'll let..." He took a deep breath that calmed him. "Okay. Okay, you let me know. But I got to tell you, that's it. That's all there is. The place is worth five hundred thirty thousand, maybe five hundred forty...and that's before you started ripping out the interior. Now, all fucked up like this..." He scowled at the clutter of construction debris. "This way, it's worth way less. And we're still willing to go six hundred kay. You hear that? Not five-forty, or even five-ninety-five. *Six hundred!* But the offer's good for a week. No more. One week, then we start looking for another place. Think *that* over!"

"I will." Wince watched Jones stride out. Pretty good exit. He hadn't known the man had it in him.

$ **32** $

Most of all, Files was sick of getting screwed over. When the old man needed something done he couldn't handle himself, who'd he ask to do it? Files. Mr. Tedescu said keep David safe, when nobody was looking to off him anyway. So here Files was, baby-sitting David, a pussy in his thousand-dollar suit and manicure. Or if Mr. Tedescu wanted somebody thumped, who did he tell take care of it?

And when it was all done, then what? No 'thank you.' No salary or commission, not even what salesmen call a "draw." He got handouts. Mr. Tedescu would drop a couple bills on him. Never all that much. Only one time five hundred, the night he took out the asshole from Miami who got caught trying to run in some shaved dice on the hundred-dollar table.

Except for some handouts—use the basement gym when he wanted, maybe hump one of the house girls—the whole deal stunk. Charity! He'd be better off driving a truck.

But there wasn't much he could do. He sat by the phone, where he'd been waiting since 6:00.

It was almost ten when Mr. Tedescu finally phoned. "Is that you Artie?"

Sometimes, for a smart rich guy, that Mr. Tedescu acted kind of retarded. Who else was going to answer Files's phone? "Yeah, it's me. I'm waiting right here. Where I called you from, right at six on the dot."

"Shut up, Artie. I'm sending you a list of all the people Tee Jay's met with there in Albuquerque. Or Window Rock. Anyone he's talked to. Wherever he's been. You check the list and add any missing names and have it ready by tonight. Do you understand?"

"Uh…'understand'…what?"

"The list, Artie. Read it and add to it anyone who's missing. Clear?"

"One list for all the names, or different lists for each one? There's been maybe ten, fifteen people he talked to down here. Some of them you can't count. I mean, you probly shouldn't count waitresses, and you can't buy a beer without talking to the bartender, you know?"

"I'm sending you *one* list, Artie. Only one. Forget bartenders and serving people."

"Whyn't you ask Tee Jay to check the names? He knows them better than—"

"Artie? Artie, listen to me. I want this done without Tee Jay's knowledge. Is that a problem for you?"

He could see *El Gato Negro* out the window and decided to go get a beer. As soon as this conversation was over. "No Sir, Mr. Tedescu."

"Artie! Two of my men did some checking in Window Rock, then spent the last week in Albuquerque, following Tee Jay. They compiled the list."

"What two men? I never seen no two men."

There was a pause. "That was the point, Artie. You didn't see them. Tee Jay didn't see them. Today you *will* see them.

He will not! Augment the frigging list, if you can, and follow their instructions. Do what they tell you!"

"Yessir, Mr. Tedescu." This time he did understand. "Are they guys I know? Maybe McMahon and Little Jerry?"

"You don't know them."

"Then how can I tell if—"

"Artie, I'm growing impatient. *Listen!* Only two men will come to your room this afternoon. Wait for them. Follow their instructions." Mr. Tedescu hung up.

So there it was. Screwed again. How was he supposed to work in the dark? People he didn't know, with a job that made no sense. Mr. Tedescu's two men...screw 'em. No way Files was going to hang around his hotel room waiting for two guys, he didn't know them from Adam. He went to grab a beer.

"Draft three contracts," Wince said. He sat on a folding chair, hunched over a mounted jackalope head resting on the seat of another chair facing him. He was trying to Superglue a loose antelope prong-horn hanging canted off the jackrabbit head. "Three contracts," he told Quintana, ticking them off on his fingers while Quintana took notes.

"One of them has me selling the restaurant, the adjacent lot, all the property, the works. The second one sells only forty-nine percent of it. Not Buck's fifty-one."

Tsosie nodded, a big smile. "Let me give you a hand." He leaned forward to hold the head while Wince reattached the loose antler.

"Thanks. Keep it steady."

Quintana said, "You selling it to Jones, personally, or to

that bunch he lobbies for? The Hispanic Economic...whatever."

"No, leave the buyer blank. We can fill it in at closing."

"That's two contracts," Quintana said. "What's the other for?"

"The sale of *Half-Off* to...whoever. Just leave the buyer blank, for now. And leave the seller blank as well."

Quintana peered at him. "You just got away from me," he said. "You're setting it up for *any*body to sell your dad's restaurant to...*anybody else*. How's that even possible? Do you mean a *re*-sale? ... You're not going to tell us, are you?"

Wince smiled. "Call it contingency planning. You never know. —How's this look?" He held up the repaired jackalope head.

"Looks natural-born," Tsosie said. "Let me hang it by the door."

"For now, leave it on the counter here."

Quintana said, "Why draw up the three contracts? Drafting even one could take a couple hours of work, for no real purpose. You saying you're selling *Half-Off* three times?"

Wince laughed. "If I could... No. Once'll do."

"You really want to sell it to Jones?"

Tsosie interrupted. "Aren't we talking about boiler-plate on these contracts? You point to your secretary, she types a name or two, pushes a computer button, and *zap*, the printer spits it out, all ready to go."

"There's more to it than that," Quintana said, and then laughed. "But not much more. —Okay, I'll draw up the contracts. You in a hurry?" he asked Wince.

"Tomorrow," Wince said. "I'll need them, at least one of them, soon."

"Which one?"

"Let me have three copies of each. And, one other thing. Aren't you a notary?"

"I was. Laura still is." He answered Wince's look. "Laura? My paralegal? You met her."

That's when T. J. David walked in. Conversation stopped.

It took Wince three or four seconds to recognize him. This wasn't the Thomas Jefferson David, Esq., of custom shirts and hand-tooled Italian shoes. Instead of flaunting Armani and Bond Street and Countess Mara or Boss, he walked in, a living billboard for Western Warehouse. Tony Lama ostrich boots, honest-to-god Levi flare jeans, Resistol shirt, silver bolo and Navajo belt buckle the size of a paperback book. Overdone, but not outrageous. No spurs, no ten-gallon hat, like Jones. Then the sun shining though the front window reflected off David's silver collar-points and made Wince reconsider 'outrageous.'

He knew that David was trying to blend in. The man wanted to deal.

"Welcome," Wince said.

"You didn't return my call."

"I knew you'd be here without that. Come on in. Would you like some coffee?"

"I would." David nodded to Quintana and Tsosie. "How goes it?"

Quintana nodded back but said nothing.

Tsosie said, "I see you did some shopping."

David shrugged. "When in Rome…"

"You're lookin' good," Tsosie said. "For a cowboy."

"Yes…?"

"I just mean, history pits cowboys against Indi'ns. If we're doing a movie scene, you're the kind of guy I better look out for. I'm an Indi'n."

"Ahhh, but you're a Mexican Indian, didn't you say?"

"Borders shift. Once New Mexico was Mexican, too."

Wince watched them, looking for tension. He decided they were playing. "Buck's *Tlaxcalan*," he said. "At least fractionally. So 'Mexican' is right."

Nodding, Tsosie said, "He knows all about that. Like I told you, Robert. Mr. David came to see me, and we talked about the gift shop here, what it's like to live on the rez, lots of things. He's heard my story. Maybe now I ought to just take off and let the three of you talk."

"Not 'three,' two of them," Quintana said. "I've got to push some buttons." He picked up his attaché case and left.

"It's almost noon. I better go spring Elliott," Tsosie said. "Maybe give him a lift home. Unless he connected with that nurse?" He looked his question at Wince.

"I don't think so. Nurses know how to chill out horny patients. They get hit on all the time."

"It's those white uniforms that do it," Tsosie said. "Sexy, you know?"

"Elliott will need a ride. And tell him I'll call."

Wince waited till the pair walked out before he poured two cups of coffee and handed one to David. "You want to have a seat?"

"Did I see that guy Jones when I was parking out front?"

That was a surprise. "You know him?"

"We've met." David put his cup down.

"He was here." Wince backed onto a stool and put his cup on the countertop, making himself small and quiet. It was David's move. Something Wince had once heard: in a negotiation, the first one to offer a number loses. Wince kept his mouth shut.

"Well… How's it going?"

"I've been better."

"You mean, the fire."

"It looks like maybe thirty thousand dollars damage, a week's work or more to clean it up."

David nodded. "Okay, sorry about that. I know that's tough, but—"

"And my partner's in the hospital."

"Chávez?"

"Yes, Chávez."

"Sorry." David chewed his lip, took a step toward the door, then turned back, standing erect, shoulders back. He offered a broad smile that failed to reach his eyes. "Maybe I can help you."

Wince nodded, waiting.

"After looking around here, I had this idea."

"Looking around…*here?*"

"Looking around Albuquerque. You know, Old Town, across the river, lots of properties." David peered at him, cautious. "You knew I've been checking out real estate, right?" At Wince's shrug he said, "Okay, so an idea came to me. There may be a way you and I could both benefit." David turned to examine the room, nodding. "Both of us."

Wince nudged him along. "Oh? What's your idea?" He leaned forward and nodded.

"Well, I might take this place off your hands, you understand?"

"Really? Did you ever run a restaurant?"

"You can own one without running it yourself."

"I guess that's true. An investment?"

David's smile was even broader, now. "Don't forget, I managed *The Shangri-La*. For six years. Besides the casino, the showroom, there was a restaurant and a coffee shop, all of them larger and more complex than..." He waved at the empty room. "Than this. Taking on a restaurant doesn't really worry me all that much, if it's a good fit for me. That's my benefit in the deal. And you...it would free you up a little. A bit of relief."

"I can think of a couple of *ifs*."

"If...?"

"*If* I decide to sell. And if you really want to pay the price."

"That might be tough. But, let's see...what number did have in mind?"

Wince looked around the room. "My dad built this place. A lot of sweat went into it. Six, seven years of work, establishing relationships with suppliers, wholesalers, hiring and training a staff, building a clientele...I don't know. He put his heart into it. How do you calculate all that? *Good will*...that has a value."

David nodded. "It does, but the place needs a lot of work to bring it back to what it was like. You know, when your father was here. But ... even the way it looks now, I'd be willing to offer...say, five hundred thousand. Or five-ten."

Wince sat back on his stool. "Ahhh, I see. Well…I'm afraid not. No deal." He rose and took his coffee cup over to the counter-back sink to dump and rinse it.

"*No?*"

"To start, it's my Dad's retirement. And I'd have to talk to Buck about it. He's a partner."

"Of course. Okay, you talk to him, see what he thinks."

"And I wouldn't bother him without a more realistic figure in mind."

"What would be more 'realistic'?"

"Let's round it up." Wince looked away, peering into the kitchen. "Say. one million."

"What the…?" David flinched. He calmed himself, opening and closing his fists. "That's *way* out of reach."

Wince smiled and turned to face him. The negotiation began.

$ 33 $

When Tsosie reached the hospital, Chávez was seated on the side of his bed, dressed. "You okay?"

"And ready to get the hell out of here."

"Okay," Tsosie said. "You want to bring the flowers?" He pointed at the bouquet sitting on the window sill. White daisies and some kind of green fronds.

"Not mine. The old timer in the other bed went home and left them. And the magazines on the table. You ever read *AARP*?"

"I look that old to you? What's it take to be an AARPer? Past fifty, I think? Or sixty? You think I look that old? Maybe I could get the senior discount at Furrs, or start going to the early bird dinners. What do you—"

"Buck? You want to shut up?" Chávez tossed the magazine to him.

"I want to take you home. Robert said—"

"Not yet." He hooked a thumb over his shoulder pointed at the hallway. "Ask them."

"Well, when you're ready, I'll give you a lift."

"My pants are here," Chávez said, hoisting a paper sack. "The shaving gear Bob brought. Only I'm not going till Chutters decides I can."

"Chutters? The cop?"

Detective Chutters walked in, looking at the notepad

he carried. "I need to get a couple things sorted out before Chávez here takes off."

"Yeah?" Chávez stood and shuffled from one foot to the other. "You want to know did I recognize the firebug, ¿qué no?"

"We're past that," Chutters said. "I'm looking for Files. The Vegas guy?"

Chávez shook his head. "Haven't seen him. Maybe you remember, I been here two days, and he didn't come visit. You see him anywhere here?" Chávez indicated the two empty beds, the one nearer the window with its sheets pulled tight. Chávez's paper sack sat atop the tangled bedclothes of the other.

"Tsosie?" Chutters still held the notepad, waiting. "You know Files. Where's he hanging out?"

"He's following his boss around. David. As far as I know. Why? You think he's the fire setter?"

"He's a person of interest in several cases."

Chávez said, "Tell you what. I get out of here, I'll tell him you want him, case I run into him."

"What's the chance of that?"

"He's staying at the Hilton over on University. If I was some high-powered detective, you know, like you are, maybe I'd search for him where he lives."

Chutters looked at him for a moment. "Always the smart-ass, aren't you? He's not there. Checked out yesterday."

"What do you want him for?" Tsosie asked.

Chutters tucked his notebook into a jacket pocket. "If you see him, call me." He handed them both a business card.

"He's a bad guy, huh?" Tsosie said.

Chávez said, "Dumb as a rock. He couldn't find his ass with both hands. What's he done?"

Chutters walked out without answering.

After a pause, Tsosie said, "Doesn't say much, does he?"

"I'd say I want to get out of here, before these *bobos* charge me a hundred bucks for an enema I never got, or a wart transplant." Chávez grabbed the paper sack and led the way out.

Wince found a parking space on *Los Arboles* two blocks west of Begay's Indian Arts. Saturday afternoon, the narrow residential streets of Old Town were jammed. A dozen tourists followed the mapped walking tour of Old Town, strolling along the cottonwood shaded streets. They paused to admire the hundred-year-old adobe houses, gawking over low walls and peering into open doorways at the dark interiors. They drifted in and out of the retail shops scattered along the streets—jewelry shops, boutiques with denim or buckskin or velvet in the window. Wince enjoyed the smiles his two restored houses on *Los Arboles* earned—Rolan Begay's shop, and the residence next door.

For the hundredth time he wished the new owners would repaint the damn Pepto-Bismol pink window frames. It was his restoration, and they'd turned it into gingerbread. All it needed was window boxes of plastic flowers or an Astroturf lawn!

Outside Begay's Indian Arts he stepped aside to let a pair of older women leave, then ducked inside before the door closed after them. He was feeling good. He had an invitation to deliver.

Rolan waved a greeting and motioned at the café doors that separated the shop from his living quarters in the back. He mouthed *Leela* and canted his head, sending Wince through the shop.

Wince found her sitting at the small kitchen table with a cup of tea. "I didn't think I'd see you this weekend," he said. "Sorry I couldn't drive up. It was my turn."

"It's okay."

"I didn't know you were driving down."

"I didn't either."

He tugged the room's other chair closer and sat at the table with her. "What's going on?"

"Nothing special."

"You mean, you don't want to say? Or have you and I got a problem?"

She offered a wry laugh. "*A* problem? More like a dozen problems. Each of us. For me, I've quit worrying about the casino thing. It's coming, nothing I can do about it. And my—"

"I'm not so sure of that."

"After seeing David in his own environment, I am. He's the future. I'm not."

Wince nodded and tried to frame his comment. "You're probably right, Window Rock's going to get a casino, sooner or later. But it doesn't have to be David's casino, and later's better than sooner...if somebody could make that happen. You know—delay it, if not block it."

"Okay...'*if*.' But meanwhile I'm worrying about something I can't change. I've been so preoccupied with that, I don't think I'm doing a good job with my class. The kids ought to come first. And now I find out I can't talk to Rolan anymore. He's all fired up about the casino, thinks it's the best idea since snow tires, and you... Well..."

"And I haven't been much help."

She shook her head. "I don't expect that.

We haven't even got to your dozen problems, yet. —Tell me, why are you being so good to Buck?"

"*Uh!*" The question gave him whiplash. He said, "Where'd that come from?"

"Buck's been keeping me posted on a few things. One, his partnership in the gift shop. And he said you're trying to authenticate his family tree. Why? Most people wouldn't bother."

"Buck exaggerates."

"No, that's just the kind of thing you do. With everything you've on your mind, to spend time helping Buck...I don't know if I'd involve myself in that, but that's...you."

"Hey! How are you?" Rolan bounded into the room, all energy and good cheer. "Charlene got here. She can handle any customers. You okay?"

Wince nodded. "Doing fine. What's got you pumped up?"

"David called me. Looks like Begay's Indian Arts will be opening a branch in Window Rock. At the new casino."

"Really?" Wince looked at Leela for confirmation.

She only shrugged. "Maybe. Down the road somewhere."

Rolan nodded. "You bet your bones!"

Wince held up a hand to stem the enthusiasm. "Before you explain that, I came to invite you to dinner. Tuesday night, *High Finance*, at seven."

"*High Finance*? What's the big occasion?"

"A ceremony of sorts. Maybe a celebration.

Five of us. Leon and I, the two of you, and we're repaying David's hospitality, maybe teaching him what Hatch chile is all about."

"Okay!" Rolan said. "We'll take him up on the tram?"

"Or meet him there."

Leela pushed back from the table. "Tuesday? I don't think so. I've got a meeting in Gallup, a fund-raiser for our computer lab."

"Can't you get out of it?" Wince asked. "Just that one night. I'd really like you there. You'll enjoy it. Good food, a couple of surprises...."

"Not mid-week," she said. "The drive's too much."

Wince knew begging wouldn't do any good. Before he could devise a persuasive argument, Rolan had started his recital of his latest successes with the Begay Inventory Association. Wince watched Leela walk through the café doors out into the gift shop. He also knew that if he followed, he'd see her leaving the shop.

$ 34 $

Files and two of Mr. Tedescu's employees were parked out-side the Hilton. Both employees were bulky, both blond, both strangers to Files. Although he didn't know their names, they resembled pro linemen he had known. The trio intercepted David when he stepped out of a Yellow cab and started into the lobby.

"David! Over here!" Files beckoned.

"What do—"

"Shut up and get in the car." The shorter tackle seized his arm to spin him around and push him toward a black limo. "Mr. Tedescu says come with us."

"Get your hands off me." David jerked free but the tight end seized his arms from the back and pushed him sprawl-ing into the back seat of the car. They crowded into the car to wedge in on either side of him, pinning him in place.

Files slid behind the wheel.

They took David to the Albuquerque Sunport and Mr. Tedescu's plane. No one spoke.

David asked for an explanation but no one answered. They flew to Las Vegas.

David followed Files into Mr. Tedescu's office. Sheree was at her desk, looking smug. David felt as if he was being "deliv-ered." The silence from his escorts grated on him. They'd

238

offered no explanation for descending on him like kidnappers. Mr. Tedescu had ordered him home, that was it. David knew the next few minutes promised nothing good.

Get past the few minutes, he'd still have to work the stupid hunky. His agreement with Wince was straightforward enough, but getting Mr. Tedescu to provide start-up funds without explaining all the details would be tough. David tried ignoring his escort—Files ahead of him, the two bodyguards or whatever they were flanking him—and focused on the pitch he'd started to rehearse on the plane.

Mr. Tedescu's garb threw David off balance before a word was said. Gold today, head-to-foot. Or maybe yellow. Bolder and brighter than lemon. It was less a color than a light show. He'd even put a gold rinse in his hair. The man glowed.

Mr. Tedescu whispered something but David didn't get it. "Yes?"

"You have silver points on your collar, Tee Jay. Are they part of the shirt, or accessories added after dressing?"

"My shirt?" David looked down at his costume. Western Warehouse didn't work here.

"Silver's ass," Files said. "They're tin! You can get them anywhere. I seen—"

"Stay out of it, Artie." Mr. Tedescu lurched to his feet to stand towering over them. "Enough! The three of you, you may leave," he said, waving them away. "I want to see Tee Jay alone."

"Yes sir," Files said. "You said bring him. We went and found where he was. We dragged his ass straight here. I got to say, he didn't want to come. He was—"

"Artie. Take a walk. Now. Not another word." Mr. Tedescu

shot his shirt cuffs and waited till only David stood before him.

When the two were alone, his mood changed and he softened. "Come on Tee Jay, smile. Come have a seat." He gestured at the single chair beside his glass-top table, then sat again on his throne. "Where are we?"

David ran through his progress with the Begays and the likelihood that Malcolm Obee had already recruited a fraction of the council sympathetic to the idea of a casino. Or interested in the chance of a payoff. He was positive, factual, and optimistic. And after he'd reassured Mr. Tedescu that their managing a casino in Window Rock was not only possible but probable, he trotted out his surprise. Plan B.

"But," he said. "As good as that opportunity is, I don't see it paying off in less than three years. A year to plan and negotiate the details, a year's construction, and four to six months decorating, equipping, staff-training. Call it thirty months from the day the council says 'go.'"

"Thirty months? I was depending on you Tee Jay. You're my boy. You're smart, and I thought you could work smart. I expected that you'd bring me good news. But you haven't." He turned away to pick up a sheet of notepaper lying on his desk. David knew it was a ploy. He waited, said nothing.

After a long moment, Mr., Tedescu looked up from the paper, feigning surprise at seeing David still there. "Yes?"

"Thirty months, but... In the meantime, I've turned up another opportunity that can pay off for us in three to four months. With a huge upside in the next year. It's a property I've been negotiating to buy. Not build, not even remodel.

Buy! Buy outright, and simply decorate. We move table games and slots into an adequate, existing space. Staff up, and cash in. No showroom, but that's a plus. It's a perfect location."

"Where?"

"In the center of Albuquerque, at the junction of the two major interstates."

"It takes more than location. Getting licensed will—"

"Taken care of," David said. "It's Indian owned, already BIA approved as a site. I've seen the certificate. Framed and hanging there."

"Is this the Wince restaurant?" Mr. Tedescu accepted David's nod and said, "Why is Wince willing to sell?"

"He doesn't know what a goldmine he has on his hands. He's thinking about running a pair of old cranker slots in his little gift shop. *Two!*"

"You said he's smart. Perhaps not."

"About some things, yes. About casinos…I don't think so."

Mr. Tedescu said, "When a deal looks too good to be true, it's… You know the rest of that."

"This time it's better than true. You met Wince."

"I met him as Begay's contractor friend, not the owner of a goldmine."

"That's the point. Wince knows construction. But business…? He's dumb as a post. The opportunity I see should be obvious, even to a gomer like him, but he can't see it. He thinks of the property as a failing restaurant, because that's what it's been. It's a perfectly adequate building with a small coffee shop, great parking on the property, wonderful location, right in the center of town. There's no licensed casino inside the city limits. It's a real treasure! And he's agreed to sell it to me."

"When have you had the time to work on all this?" Mr. Tedescu looked at the hand-written list he held in one hand. "Wince, is it?"

"Yes sir."

"Who is…" He peered at the list. "This man Quintana. Leon Quintana."

"He's nobody. A small-time lawyer and accountant, nobody special."

"Uh-huh. And this one, Elliott Chavéz?"

"I think it's pronounced *Chávez*." David flinched. Correcting Mr. Tedescu wouldn't get him anywhere. "Sorry," he said. "Chávez is another contractor, works with Wince." David leaned closer to look at the list. "Why ask about him?"

Mr. Tedescu shook his head. "And this Wince is going to sell you his restaurant, for how much?"

"We started miles apart. I offered half-a-mil, he said a million."

"A million dollars? A frigging *million!?*"

"That's what he said, but it's ridiculous. He just blurted out the number. He's never seen that much money. It's the contractor in him, going for a homerun. So I worked him. It took some dickering but we finally settled at eight hundred—five hundred thousand up front, nothing per month, with an interest-free three hundred thousand balloon at the end of two years. He'll carry it at principal-only that long."

Mr. Tedescu nodded, and mumbled, and jotted down something on the paper he held, and said, "What's your

source? Do you have five hundred thousand? Or a fairy god-
father?"

David knew the question was rhetorical. Or a challenge.
He refused to be baited.

"You think I should wave my wand? Half a million dollars,
on top of what you already owe me? How likely do you think
that is?" Mr. Tedescu leaned back in his chair and waited for
David's answer. This time the question wasn't rhetorical.

The hunky was holding his breath.

Prepared, David laid out his proposition. He was calm,
in control. This was his strength, to know what the old man
wanted to hear and to allow the answers to be pulled from
him one at a time. Each answered question laid a paving
stone in the path he was constructing. The path to his future.

It took eight minutes.

In eight minutes, they agreed. Mr. Tedescu would provide a cashier's check for $500,000. David would meet Wince
for closing on Tuesday evening, three days hence. He would
guide the furnishing and preparation of the Albuquerque *Shangri-La Casino*, and manage it when it opened. At
the same time, he would pursue the opportunity in Window Rock, with no benefit accruing to him from that site,
no matter what success it might enjoy. Mr. Tedescu would
receive 80% of the net from the Albuquerque *Shangri-La*
until David had repaid his debt of $2,000,000. (*Two million,
to repay a-million-five!*). From that moment on, the Albuquerque *Shangri-La* would belong, free and clear, to Tee Jay
David and the limited corporation he planned to create. Free
and clear, but for a "royalty" of 8% of the net to Mr. Tedescu,
monthly, for the term of his life.

That's it. All the terms.

"Except..." Mr. Tedescu said, in his softest whisper, "If we're not settled up three years from today, I will disappear you."

"No problem." David reached out to shake Mr. Tedescu's hand.

"Not yet. Bring me the deed of title and a pro forma on opening costs, then we'll shake on it.

Now, when is the closing?"

"Tuesday evening, seven pee em, at a restaurant called *High Finance.*"

"At night? For a business meeting?"

David shrugged. "Wince is making a big deal of it. His Indian partner thinks there's some magic up on that mountain. Something like that. So we'll sign the contracts at dinner, Tuesday night."

"Here we are, dealing with some frigging cowboy." Mr. Tedescu sighed. "Okay then. I'll have your check ready downstairs at reception."

David started for the door but was stopped before he reached it.

"One thing," the hunky said. "When you're in Albuquerque again, pick me up a pair of silver collar points like yours. Silver, not tin."

"Yes sir. I'll be glad to."

Mr. Tedescu had to get the last word. "I like you Tee Jay. I always have. But, if there are any problems, you become... a ghost. *Poof!*" He waved him away.

David smiled at Sheree on his way past her desk.

Little structural damage. None from the fire. The only real destruction was the result of firemen's axes. But the stench was still here. It would take some time to clear that away. And Wince knew he couldn't bring back the buyers of the other units till the smell was gone, or diminished. He sat on an overturned bucket and jotted down reminders to himself. The plumbing in 4 and 6 was okay, but the wiring in the walls would have to be checked and probably replaced. Water damage to the retail units on the first floor was mainly cosmetic. He'd get Charlene Bosco and her boy back in here to paint and clean up. Wince managed a wry smile. The stink of fresh paint would seem like perfume.

"Not as bad as I thought," Chávez said, coming down the stairs from the second floor units.

"Three walls, windows and doorways, replace the floor where the firemen went nuts. I make it close to twenty thousand, everything in. Not as bad as I thought."

"No, Bobby. *Creo* fifteen, *no mas*. Let me rip out the walls up there and see, to be sure."

"Do what you can," Wince said. "I got us a few days delay from Sanchez, and come Wednesday morning we'll have the cash to get him off our back."

Chávez clapped him on the shoulder. "Hey, man, I'm sorry it came to that. Selling your restaurant, just to bail us out here."

"Every problem creates an opportunity."

"Now you're a philosopher, is that it?"

Wince stood. "I'm doing okay. *Half-Off*'s taking care of itself. Our main worry now is, can you get the guys back in here to help clean this up?"

"Not Stapely, not after we fired his ass. But Larry Gonzalez and Wheezer said they'll come in tomorrow. We'll get it done. I'll fix it. You sell it."

"Deal!" They slapped hands and Wince went out to buy supplies…from any retailer who would extend him credit.

David felt free. He'd come back to Albuquerque on his own, without Files tagging along this time. He had Sunday ahead of him to complete planning, if he could get Wince to open the restaurant, maybe give him the key. He had a mental image of the floor layout he wanted but had to take some measurements before he could firm up a plan. He'd already contacted Amusements Inc. and had Al Gordoni working up cost sheets on gaming-machine rentals. It was coming together. He sat at his fourth floor window in the Hilton. He'd never checked out, so he still had the same room. Familiar surroundings helped calm him. Files was gone, another plus. Mr Tedescu had relaxed his death-grip on his wallet and provided the check now tucked into the breast pocket of David's new corduroy sports coat. Life was good.

And getting better. He pictured what his casino could look like. It wouldn't be a *Shangri-La* clone. Let Mr. Tedescu think that for now, at least till David decided on a name for it. And he tried to imagine Wince's reaction to seeing it open, no longer a seedy little diner but a money-machine he'd let get away from him. David enjoyed winning. Everyone does. But not everyone gets the extra buzz of knowing the loser well enough to enjoy seeing him sweat.

If he could just keep a straight face at the closing… Sign the papers, say nothing, let Wince think whatever he wanted to. All the time, David would be savoring his victory. A real winner crushes his opponent. He and Wince were crusher, and crushee.

He called down to room service to order a Grey Goose martini and a banana split.

$ 35 $

"Is Buck on the way?" Wince asked. He and Quintana stood in the parking lot below the tram base station and waited for Rolan Begay to lock his Lincoln. Wince moved closer to peer into the parked car. Empty. "Buck's not with you?."

He watched Rolan hesitate over his answer. "Uh, . . . I guess not."

"What's up?" Quintana said.

"He drove Leela home Sunday night, and they're not back."

Both Rolan and Quintana turned to Wince.

"She asked him to take her up, right?"

Rolan nodded. "Sorry, man, but she's acting like...I don't know what."

"It's been coming."

"You going to explain that?" Quintana said.

"I don't want to miss the tram. We need to get up there. They're setting up the small dining room for us."

Rolan scanned the queue of passengers ready to board the next tram car. "What about Tee Jay?"

"He'll be there," Wince said. "No way he'd miss this evening." He climbed the creaking staircase to join the queue.

The tram flight was smooth and uneventful, crewed by a girl young enough to wear braids. The passengers were better dressed than daytime visitors Wince had seen on earlier visits. Most were headed up to enjoy dinner on the crest and

248

watch the setting sun light the western sky. Day's end cast a serene pink haze over visitors here on the Sandias' west face. Atmosphere. Buck Tsosie's "place of good consequences," the reason that Buck had asked Wince to hold the closing at *High Finance*.

Now that Buck wouldn't be there, Wince would have to report on the evening. Just as he expected that Buck—or Leela—might tell him about their evening elsewhere. *Might* tell him, but might not. They were both Navajo. And he wasn't, a fact that stood between him and Leela.

The three joined the others in filing out of the tram car into the cool evening breeze and the scent of pine and piñon atop the Sandia ridge. Quintana led the way to *High Finance*. He'd chosen the menu, asked the catering manager to plan the dinner, and had paid in advance.

She met them in the doorway. "Welcome, gentlemen. Mr. David is already here. Please come in."

Rolan walked across the carpeted room to greet David, who had a drink in his hand and was standing at the west window. He was pretending to admire the view. His clenched left fist tapped a rhythm on the window sill.

Quintana pulled the catering manager aside. "My secretary says you're a notary."

"Yes sir. So is Reuben, the day manager."

"You have your seal here?"

She smiled at the question. "Always," she said. "In my office."

"We'll need you, and your seal, after dinner," Wince said.

"I'll be here with your dessert."

Wince and Quintana took their smiles across the room to

join the others. Rolan was talking. David teetered from heel to toe and fidgeted near the window.

"You beat us up here," Wince said.

"I caught the earlier tram. It was loading when I got here so I jumped on. I figured to ride up together with the rest of you, but you weren't there yet."

"Well, I'm glad you're here. How was your day?"

The small talk lasted through one beer for Wince and another martini for David. The sun was low enough that lengthening shadows of the volcanic cones on the west mesa spread their tapered paths across the valley floor below. It was clear that David—shuffling his feet, almost dancing—wanted to move along. Wince said, "They do great prime rib here."

Quintana said. "As good as the view."

"Our business will wait," Wince said. "Come have a seat." He led David to a table set for six. White tablecloth, white napkins, glowing silver and sparkling glassware. The catering manager and a waiter hovered in the corridor just outside the door. Wince motioned them into the room and took the chair across from David and watched the man chewing his lip, clenching and unclenching his fist. David was more than edgy.

"Hey Hey! I'm looking forward to this." Rolan took a seat. "What's the menu?"

Quintana said, "Prime rib, what else?"

Wince motioned to the servers and the meal began. The food was excellent. Only Rolan enjoyed it. Conversation lagged and alternated between forced pleasantries and uncomfortable silence. Wince knew the dinner might have been a mistake. The pending settlement hung over the table more threat than promise. He rushed his food, as ready as David to get this done.

When the dessert was served—*biscochitos* and sherbet— he pushed it aside and reached under his chair to draw out the attaché case he'd borrowed from Quintana. He placed it on the floor beside his chair, eager to get to it but unwilling to let David see the eagerness. He asked for the check—marked "paid in advance"—added a tip and slipped the receipt the waiter brought him into his coat pocket. The evening was winding down.

"I'm sorry Leela couldn't be here," Rolan said, finishing his sherbet. "She's a teacher and gets tied up during the week, getting classes ready, you know?"

"It's okay. You're sister's not my biggest fan," David said.

Commotion at the open door interrupted. It was two new arrivals. Unexpected arrivals, Artie Files leading the way. "I told you they'd be up here," Files said.

Wince looked up to see Files framed in the doorway, with Tedescu right behind him.

"I told you," Files boasted.

"Is one of those empty chairs for me?" Tedescu nodded to them all, left and right, a celebrity acknowledging a welcome no one had offered.

David was on his feet, squinting.

"We drove up the back road," Tedescu said. "Files had some trouble finding the way."

"Trouble?" Files said. "It wasn't *my* 'trouble.' It took us a fuckin' hour coming up that winding road. They should of built the road up the front, where the tram comes. I mean that's the straight way, 'stead of wandering all over the hills in the back there."

Wince leaned back in his chair and watched them. Quintana was poised on the edge of his seat, leaning forward like sprinter. Tedescu, dressed entirely in steel-gray, looked like an insurance salesman or a hip mortician. He was calm and intent on...on whatever had brought him here. And David had started to sweat, a sheen on his forehead.

"Mr. Tedescu," David said. "What are you doing here?"

Files nodded. "Weird, huh? You ever see him outside his office before?"

"Artie. Stand there. Without talking." Tedescu pointed at the far corner and waited till Files took his post.

Files propped himself against the wall and folded his arms. He squeezed his biceps in a regular rhythm.

Wince decided he was either exercising or playing with himself. "Welcome," he said. He asked Tedescu, "Have you eaten? We can probably stir up another plate."

"I don't require food. Only coffee. Black. Artie will get it." He pulled an empty chair to the table and dropped into it. "Have we progressed to the business of the evening? — Artie? Coffee. Now!"

Files made a face but looked around for a coffee pot. The catering manager motioned him still and pointed the waiter to the table, where the man filled the cup Tedescu held out to him.

"Uh, not yet," David said. "We were just getting to it."

"You didn't come six hundred miles to watch us sign a contract," Wince said.

"I could use some of that coffee," Files said.

But Tedescu raised a hand to motion him to his corner. Files slouched back to stand waiting. David looked from one to another. Tension crackled around them. Wince wanted to yawn. Quintana had settled back in his chair to watch, wide-eyed. Only Rolan was smiling.

Tedescu sipped at his coffee and set the cup down. "I've had some of my associates doing a bit of research," he said. "You've decided to sell your father's restaurant to Tee Jay. That's of course up to you. Tee Jay has described the facilities to me, and my associates confirm his description."

"What associates?" David said. "I didn't know—"

"I'm speaking." Tedescu raised a hand to silence David. "Good.... As I was saying, the property is not worth what you're asking. That's fine. I can understand such a negotiating stance. It's not worth what you're asking, but may potentially be worth more to a new owner than you recognize." He turned to David. "Isn't that how you put it, Tee Jay?"

"That's not exactly how—"

"It's *exactly* how you put it. So, I stand between these two differing evaluations, and I'm here to resolve the contradiction." He held out his hand. "Tee Jay? Give me back my check."

Wince watched David turn pale. The sweat stood out on his forehead and his hands trembled. He looked like a boy about to cry.

Files laughed, then covered his mouth and faked a cough.

David glared at him and drew an envelope from his pocket. He held it out to Tedescu.

"This is a cashier's check for half-a-million dollars." Tedescu smiled at Wince, waving the envelope. "It's yours, as Tee Jay promised, as soon as we sign the contract."

Wince reached into the attaché case on the floor beside him and drew out the contracts.

"As soon as *I* sign the contract," David said. He took a step toward Tedescu. "This is my deal! I worked it! If I—"

"Quiet, Tee Jay. I'll take care of you."

"Why are you even here? I had this all worked out, and you're screwing it up!"

Tedescu beckoned to Files and said, "Sit him down."

"Yes sir!" Files took David by the shoulders and pushed him back into his chair. He stood over him, smirking.

Wince filled in his name on two copies of the sales contract and slid the papers over to Quintana, who looked them over, nodded, and said, "What's the name and tax I.D. of the purchaser?"

"Let me do it." Tedescu filled in the blank on one copy of the contract, then the second, saying as he wrote, "Orlon Tedescu...and there's my social." He wrote for a moment longer before sliding the papers across the table to Quintana. "You're the lawyer?" he said.

"Leon Quintana."

"You'll notice that I changed the purchase price there." He pointed at a number inserted on the form. "Have Mr. Wince initial it."

Quintana held it up to read it. He flinched but said nothing. He handed it to Wince.

Wince read it, looked at Tedescu—who was nodding—and said "Really." He looked at David, then initialed the insertion, smiling. He beckoned to the catering manager.

She stepped forward to emboss both contracts with her seal and scribble on the pages.

Tedescu posed, basking in the admiration he assumed was in the offing. "For a deal to be good, both parties have to benefit. That number should make us both happy."

David said, "What are you doing?"

"I topped your bid," Tedescu said. "Eight hundred, wasn't that the agreed price? Well now it's one million dollars, Mr. Wince's asking price…albeit inflated."

He turned to Wince. "The property is worth less than you asked," Tedescu said. "But more than you know. And I'll recover the difference …elsewhere." He smiled at Wince and handed over the envelope he'd taken from David. "My first cashier's check.

"*And*…another one, just like it." He passed over a second check.

"Holy shit! One million dollars!" Files said. "Can I see that?"

Wince tucked the second check into the envelope with the first. The envelope went into his pocket.

"You don't want to examine the check?"

"It looked like a cashier's check."

Tedescu nodded.

"I appreciate it. Thank you,." Wince said.

Tedescu said, "You're really just a carpenter?" He was watching Wince for some reaction.

Nothing.

"I told you that!" David lurched to his feet again. "What about our deal?"

Tedescu waved him silent.

"*Your* deal!" Files said. "Kiss my ass, *your* deal. Without me, there *ain't* no deal!"

Wince and Quintana exchanged a glance but said nothing.

Rolan said, "*Hoo* boy! One million dollars! Buck really missed it."

Tedescu finished his coffee. He scrubbed his hands as if washing them, then said, "Let me explain, Tee Jay. I just bought the property you located. You don't owe me for that. Only one mil for your earlier...problem. And this is how you'll repay me. You'll manage the 'restaurant.'" He glanced at Wince, then winked at David. "Manage it, on salary. When your debt to me is repaid, you'll become my partner in the project." He waved as if shooing flies. "We can calculate the percentages later. But I'd say, in three or four years, you'll work off what you owe me, and I'll sell you a share in *The Albuquerque Shangri-La.*"

"*Sell* me a share? I'm the one who deserves—"

"*Hey!*" Files stepped between them. "When do I get mine?"

Tedescu shook his head. "Go wait in the car, Artie."

"I'm not waiting in no car. We wouldn't even be here if I didn't take charge. 'Tee Jay pussy' here, he was letting stuff slide when all he had to do to finish up was get Wince so fucked up he had to sell. I did that! I torched the motel. David couldn't get off the dime. It was me done—"

"I told you to wait in the car." Tedescu said. "Don't make me angry, now. Just—"

Files jerked out his Glock and fired into the floor at Tedescu's feet. "Shut up! Shut the fuck up!" The room rang with the shot. "Get over there, by your errand boy." He waved the automatic and herded them all across the room.

Wince raised both hands chest-high and spoke quietly. "Okay, take it easy. Nobody's been hurt. We can still—"

"Shut up!" Two more shots into the ceiling brought down a shower of plaster. "You don't talk. You listen!" He pointed the gun at Tedescu. "Ten shots," he said. "Seven left. You want one? Any body want one?" He threatened them all with the waving automatic and shouted louder.

The catering manager and both waiters crouched in fear.

"First one out of line, I blow his head off! Believe it." Files motioned them all aside, all but Wince.

"You," he said, beckoning with the gun. "Let's have it."

"What's that?"

"In your pocket." He thumped Wince on the chest with the gun. "A million dollars. *Now!*"

Wince drew out the envelope and handed it to him. "Be calm, now. We can—"

"Shut up! The rest of you, stay right here. You, Wince, you're coming with me." He pushed Wince toward the door. "Anyone follows us, I kill him. And you!"

Leon Quintana made the effort. "Files, you're trapped up here, on top of the mountain. No matter how you try to get down, the cops'll be waiting. If you—"

"Shut your mouth!" Files shot him.

The round hit Quintana high in the shoulder and spun him bleeding to the floor.

"Over here!" Wince shouted, throwing his coffee cup at Files as he lunged for the gun.

Files was faster. He slashed Wince across the face with

the weapon, tearing open his forehead and spinning away, screaming, "Back! Stay back!" He waved the gun over their heads.

Wince dropped to one knee. Blood from his forehead ran into his eyes, and he choked at in the stench of burnt gunpowder settling over his head like a rancid cloud. Before he could stand, Files jerked him erect and pushed him stumbling over Quintana, lying on the floor with blood staining the carpet black under him. Files screamed and shoved Wince from the room.

$ **36** $

Files knew Wince might be right. It could be a bitch, getting off this mountain, for somebody else. Not for him. Driving down was out. It'd take an hour. The tram took almost half that. Either way, a phone call to the tram station down below or police summoned to the road side of the mountain would set a trap. He saw a man in the doorway peering out into the hallway at them. And by now every diner in the restaurant with a cell was punching in 911.

Files had already figured his way out of both possibilities. Mr. Tedescu and all these hotshots, maybe they were book-smart, but they way under-estimated Artie Files. He had his ticket out. Wince. Stumbling along ahead of him.

And now he had maybe five minutes till some moron in the restaurant, whoever had balls enough, would come after him. They'd probly already reached the cops..

He goaded Wince along, not outside into the deepening darkness where searchers would expect him to go but down the corridor, to the right. Into the locker room. It stunk of sweat socks and sweet sawdust.

"Which is yours?" Files said. He pushed Wince toward the wooden lockers, vented closets made of one-by-three rough-cut boards. Their open slots, probly to let air circulate over the contents, also let him see inside them through the gaps.

Wince wiped blood out of his eyes and said, "Number six."
He touched the door.

"Open it."

Wince spun the combination and pulled the lock from the
door hasp. The door swung open.

"Get the chutes. Both chutes."

"It won't do you—"

"Get 'em!"

Wince carried the chutes. Files pushed him outside and
circled the building till they could see the silhouette of the
tram docking station against the glow of Albuquerque's
lights on the night sky. He could hear shouting from inside
the restaurant.

Wince recognized where they were headed. "Come on,
Files. Listen to me. Think about it. If you take the tram,
they'll be waiting for you. Just give it up. You haven't done
anything, yet."

Files laughed. "Sure I have." He drew the wrinkled envelope out of his hip pocket and waved it. "Stole a million
bucks. Cashiers' checks. Negotiable. Worst comes to worst I
can lay them off, you know? You think it's not worth taking a
chance for a million bucks?"

"Give it up."

"I'm not taking the tram, but neither will nobody else." He
pushed Wince forward.

Mike Baca yawned and stretched. His final flight of the
day. That chick on the last flight down with him, "Lois," she
said she'd wait for him. He checked his watch, tough to see in
the tram car's dim overhead light. By the time he got back to

the base, completed his log, washed up and checked out…35 or 40 minutes. He gave the window a last swipe with his wet rag, cleaning up. Maybe she'd wait, maybe not.

Somebody pounded at the door.

"Couple minutes!" Baca said. "Wait in the…" It was some crazy with a gun! The door slid open.

"You're in the wrong place, partner. There's no money—"

The man leaned in and laid the muzzle against the tram radio and fired. The radio danced in a shower of sparks that flared around them.

"*Jesus, man!*" Baca said. "You crazy? If you—"

But the guy was gone. Like that fast.

Blinded by the shower of sparks, Baca squinted to look for the gunman, and found him. He watched the man step to the back of the car and fire two rounds at the pulley atop the tram car. The gun barked twice and the shots ricocheted whining into the dark. Baca couldn't see what had been hit. He didn't care. He dropped sprawling to the floor and hunkered in a corner, waiting for the maniac to leave.

That did it. He was quitting this *pinche* job!

Running north away from the tram docking station, Wince knew where they were headed. He slowed to a trot, the two chute packs bouncing off his back. They were awkward and more, a useful excuse. A reason not to run as fast as Files demanded. Wince needed time to think. He tried to figure a way to stop Files. But Files still held the gun. And it still held three rounds. Wince's imagination churned but nothing occurred to him, no way of proceeding, nothing that wouldn't turn Files berserk.

The gunfire would spur someone—a dozen someone's at dinner in High Finance—to phone police. Help was on the way...not soon enough.

And if Files was trapped here atop the mountain, everyone nearby was in danger from him until he was gone. Till he was dragged off in cuffs, or escaped.

They rounded a turn in the dirt path, trotting now, away from lights of the restaurant and tram dock. Only moonlight and the ambient glow from Albuquerque below lit their way. The shale shelf hung out over the valley below. Files's plan was obvious.

"Which is better, your chute or the lawyer's."

"You mean 'safer?' They're both the same."

"Safer's ass! Which one do you jump?"

Wince shrugged, thinking quickly.

"I didn't hear you. Which one?" Files leveled the Glock at Wince's face.

"You'd be a fool to jump with either one of them. You'll kill yourself down there."

"Uh-huh. You say. You think I can't do anything you and your pussy friend done? — Just tell me, which is your chute."

Wince held out his chute at arm's length, swinging from his grip.

"Good. But I think you're one tricky dude, so I'll take the other one." Files laughed at his own cleverness and wrenched the second chute off Wince's shoulder.

"I'm telling you, you'll kill yourself."

"I see the lit-up tennis court there and the grassy place is right next to it. Looks big enough to me. I can do it."

"In the dark? You're crazy! You've never jumped before."

"Three times, I told you." Files strapped on the chute, careful to keep his gun hand free as he did. He trained the gun on Wince. "Just 'cause you're chickenshit…Well, I been sayin', I ain't you!"

"I'm just telling you, I won't jump here."

"You will if I tell you to." Files snickered. "Put on the chute. That one." He pointed. "The one you wanted to stick me with. Jump it, or I'll shoot your ass." He waved the gun.

They heard shouting back along the path.

Someone was coming.

"Now!" Files said. He glanced back toward the tram station, thinking, shuffling his feet. The voices were louder, closer. "Shit!" he said, and turned to run toward the jump off. He held the pilot chute and slider in one hand, with the other raised the gun and fired at Wince, turning as he did to run headlong out over the shale shelf and launch himself into the dark.

The bullet's impact tore the dangling chute from Wince's hand. "*Files!*" He reached for him too late and tripped over Quintana's chute to sprawl in the gravel. And then Files leapt into the darkness out of sight.

Wince scrambled to his feet, whirled and ran back toward the restaurant, counting under his breath as he punched a number into his cell phone, "Thirteen seconds, fourteen, fifteen…"

That was it. Enough time. Files was down by now. Dead or alive.

Wince stopped to lean over and catch his breath. He rested a hand on his knee and listened to Chutters answer his phone. "Dan Chutters. Who's—"

"If you want Files, get a car out to the Northside Tennis Courts, fast!"

"Wince? Is this Bob Wince? Where are—"

"Shut up, Dan! Files set the fire. Whatever else you're looking at him for, I don't know. But he did the fire. You want him? Go pick him up, Northside Tennis Courts …if he's still there. He can't get far. He's on foot."

"What are you talking—"

"Do it!" Wince snapped the phone shut.

He stopped in the corridor outside the dining room to take another deep breath, calming himself. His hand was wet, where he'd braced himself against his knee. Here, in the light, he saw the blood. He'd torn his pants in the gravel. His left knee was bleeding. Commotion inside the room told him people were coming.

Two waiters were helping Rolan carry Leon Quintana from the room. He was conscious and in pain but able to raise a hand to Wince.

Wince nodded, and watched them carry Quintana out. The catering manager was on her phone, summoning help. So was a man in seersucker shouting into his phone in the hallway.

Tedescu and David stood near the rear doorway. They spoke to each other too softly for Wince to hear, whispering. They drifted toward the door, paused, till Tedescu laid a palm on David's back, and pushed. Out the door. They were gone.

Wince snatched a napkin off the table and swabbed at his bleeding knee, brushing small pebbbles from the seeping wound. He flinched and sucked in a quick breath. His knee stung! He grimaced, listening to the gabble of conversation as Quintana was carried away.

Then he was alone in the room. He checked his breast pocket. An envelope was still there. *The* envelope. All right, okay. Not the way he'd planned it, but…okay. After all his preparations, then this fluke…but it could still….

If he handled it right….

Starting tomorrow, David would be busy enough with *Half-Off* to ignore Window Rock as a site. He'd have enough grief, trying to cobble together a hybrid casino out of a dozen ill-suited fragments, in an unauthorized Albuquerque site. A Jackalope Casino, at best.

Maybe not ideal, for David. But he was a clever guy; he might even make it work.

For others, it was near-perfect. Something for everyone. For Chávez, Tsosie, Begay…and for Wince: an even, honest million for a property appraised at four-hundred-sixty-five thousand. One million dollars, in two checks, in a single white envelope.

Wince tugged the envelope out of his pocket. Still there, two crisp cashier checks. He wondered how much Files could get by "laying off" the receipt for tonight's dinner. If he'd survived base-jumping the Sandia Ridge.

Time to compose his story. The cops would be here soon. But not Chutters.

$ 37 $

The drive from Albuquerque to Elephant Butte covered 152 miles, according to the Buick's odometer. A surveyor's dirt trail around the south end of the lake added another 12. By the time Chutters reached Wince's cabin his back was tight, and he was ready to walk off the stiffness. He left his weapon and belt under the front seat, locked the car, and went searching on foot. He found Wince beside the house, chopping wood. Bare to the waist, tanned as dark as the adobe house behind him.

"Hello Detective. Kind of out of your territory."

"'Dan.' Dan Chutters." He held out his hand

"Okay. 'Dan.' … I know." They shook hands.

"My day off. I thought I'd take a ride."

"Pretty long ride." Wince smiled and one-handed his axe high overhead to swing it down and bury the blade in the stump he was splitting. He backed away and bowed, his hand extended palm up, to offer Chutters the axe. "Give it a try?"

"Looks like a lot of work."

"I heard a retired secret service man once talk about chopping wood with Jimmy Carter. They say he chopped wood for an hour a day, till he was harder than the axe blade. No faking it. The secret service men half Carter's age couldn't keep up with him."

"You think you could have?"

"I guess I'll never know.

"But you'd like to, right?—You're a real competitive guy."

"Not on this, unless Guiness publishes log-splitter records. I'm just curious.—Look over there." Wince pointed at a huge cottonwood on the edge of the mesa overlooking the lake. It was lightning split and leaned at a steep angle, roots torn loose and exposed to the air. "It's that tree I'm competing with, next. I'm guessing I'll get eight or ten cords of firewood out of that big sucker there."

"Then what?"

Wince shook his head. "Hard to say. Stack the wood, find another tree. Something'll turn up.—I'm done with the house, except for sealing that old water tank on the roof. And the barn still needs some work."

"You've been doing the work yourself."

"Nobody has offered to help. —How 'bout you?"

"I just drove down to tie off some loose ends."

Wince walked over to a dripping gunny sack hanging from a tree limb in the breeze. "Nature's refrigerator." He took out two sweating cans of Rolling Rock and tossed one to Chutters. "You asking questions or bringing me answers?"

"Did you hear about Files?"

"You put him away."

"Yeah, thanks again for the phone call. —We picked him up at the tennis courts, where you said he'd be. Both ankles broken, but he was still trying to crawl away. He's one tough bastard. He spent ten minutes spitting at me."

"The man has a temper."

"Remember telling me once, he didn't know about New Mexico jails?" At Wince's nod, Chutters said, "He will now.

And no trial. He copped quick and took a deal. Assault, attempted murder…he'll do hard time, this time. Even without conviction on the rape charge he had coming."

"What's that about?"

"He raped a woman in Window Rock. But there's no witness, no one to testify, no clear evidence. But I know. The man's a rapist."

"Two weeks in Santa Fe with the big boys, he'll learn a lesson he won't enjoy."

"Yeah, well, Files is gone. But I'm curious about…other issues. Chávez runs your construction business now," Chutters said, shifting gears. "Why's your name still on the sign?"

"I kept a small interest, that's all. Elliott is the real builder. The company's really his."

"And your girlfriend, Leela Begay?"

"It's a six hour drive to Window Rock, from here, so I won't be seeing her that often."

Chutters waited.

"She and Buck are together, I guess. Buck decided he's *Diné*. Even *adopted Diné* is easier to explain than *Tlaxcalan*. And easier to spell."

"So you do keep up with them, even this far away."

"Buck's building their *hogan*, I hear, and helping her raise money for that computer lab she was after."

"You know they're getting married?" Chutters pressed.

"It wouldn't surprise me. —But that's not the reason you're here, checking up on my ex-girl-friends."

Chutters balanced his empty beer can on a stump. "None of this is personal. But I do have a couple questions." He waited. "Okay?"

"Another beer?"

"Confirm some numbers for me," Chutters said, shaking his head 'no.' He took a small notebook from his shirt pocket and flipped it open. "You sold your father's restaurant to that Vegas millionaire, Files's boss, a mister..." He consulted the notebook. "...mister Orlon Tedescu. Sold it for one million dollars."

"That's a lot of money. I could sure use it."

"Where is it?"

"You know that already. Files took it. Four or five witnesses saw it all. Tedescu got his restaurant, I got shafted. One million bucks, gone! All I get out of it is a lesson."

"And your construction company, with your name on it, gets to write-off the loss."

"*Some* of it. Not all."

"So it's you being lucky again," Chutters said.

"You think that's the end of it? Where's the money? Two cashier's checks! How lucky's that?"

"Files says you pulled a switch."

"Sure he does. I'd say that same thing, in his shoes. He stashed them somewhere, before you picked him up."

"Somewhere within crawling distance?" Dan Chutters waited. "No. All I know, he 'lost' them...if he ever had them."

"Careless." As Wince talked he drifted in a semi-circle to his left, turning Chutters, facing him, as well. "You don't think I... You could check with my bank, I guess. 'Follow the money.' Isn't that a cop saying?"

"I checked. It's not in your bank."

Wince smiled. "You found your way into my bank account? Legally?"

"Well, I've got friends. They checked for me, and you don't have it. At least not where I can find it. And no safe deposit box. —I know, I know. It was a crazy couple of hours that night. There was a lot of confusion, diversions, misdirection. Maybe it was pure cleverness."

"Somebody clever enough to fool those Las Vegas sharpies?"

Chutters nodded. "Yeah, maybe you."

"No, no, that's way too complicated for me. Ask David. He'll tell you."

"There's more. Little more than a month later, Tedescu sold *Half-Off*. Again. Only now it's called *Dos Chicas*. The buyer was Albuquerque's own Tom Jones. And who arranged the sale? You did!" Chutters wiped a wet hand on his pants. "See why I need help untangling all this?"

Wince nodded. "I guess Tedescu decided the restaurant wasn't right for him. A misunderstanding. David must have seen some potential that wasn't really there."

"So he sold it to Jones?"

"Actually, not Toe-MAS himself. The organization Jones works for bought it."

By this time, Chutters had turned through a semi-circle and was looking directly into the sun. He blinked and said. "You handled the sale."

"Uh-huh. What's your question?"

"Tedescu sold it for six hundred kay and took a four hundred thousand dollar loss."

"Maybe not really. You know what the casinos tell you. It's not a loss, if it pays the cost of your entertainment. You have to buy your 'Fun.' Maybe Tedescu considered it the cost of entertainment?"

"A week's entertainment...for four hundred kay?"

"He was very entertained." As they talked, Wince drifted under the shade of the cottonwood. "He also expects that David will make it up and repay him."

"Why David?"

"Buying *Half-Off* was David's idea, and he already owed Tedescu for something, I don't know what."

Chutters shook his head. "Then Tedescu's out of luck, because David has disappeared."

"I thought they both went back to Vegas."

"When Tedescu sold the restaurant–actually *re*-sold it— David disappeared."

"That's it? 'Disappeared'?"

"The corporation sent him to Puerto Rico, Tedescu told the Vegas Pee Dee, to manage a new casino there, only he never arrived."

"Maybe he skipped out. I don't blame him." Wince thought for a moment. "David knew not to hang around where Tedescu could get at him. He'd get out before he was got at."

"Or maybe he was 'got at' before he could get out."

"I don't know. David was one really smart guy. —You could ask him."

"Why do you say 'was'?"

"Oh, did I?"

"And it *was* you that brokered the sale for Tedescu."

"I've still got my broker's license."

"Can I ask what you got out of it?" Chutters tugged his

collar loose and looked up at the sun. Really hot today.

"Satisfaction," Wince said. "Seller and buyer were both happy."

"So you did it as a charitable act?"

"I gave Tedescu a break on my commission. Half the regular broker's fee. Three per-cent, not six. He was happy to unload the restaurant…when he decided it wouldn't work as a casino."

Chutters shook his head. "'Happy' to give you sixteen thousand dollars?"

"Eighteen."

"Oh, right. Eighteen thousand. And he was happy with that?"

"Let's say 'content.' … You have to pay for your fun."

Chutters closed his notebook and tucked it back into his shirt pocket. "That's kind of the way I ran the numbers."

"I'm glad it all worked out." Wince jerked the axe loose from the stump. … "Anything else on your mind?"

"Oh…one thing," Chutters said. "Tedescu's out four hundred kay, the million he paid you, minus the six hundred he sold the place for. You're out the million, you say. Where is it? I can't find it. It's still missing, and you seem pretty calm about it."

"What you can't change…." He shrugged.

Chutters peered at him. "I've got to wonder where it went."

"It'll probably turn up. When somebody spends it."

"And…you?"

Wince shrugged. "I've got my health."

"I see Chávez is in the black."

"Elliott's got a good business head."

"Tsosie's building a new house."

"Are the two connected?" Wince said, covering a smile.

Chutters knew Wince was enjoying the duel but kept at it. "It's going to cost Tsosie, and I don't remember him winning the lottery. What do you think is going on there?"

"He's building over near Window Rock, I hear. Not in New Mexico, Window Rock *Arizona*. ... Has APD got you working in Arizona now?"

Chutters shook his head, a faint surrender. "Got an answer for everything, don't you?"

"I try, Detective."

"It's 'Dan.'"

"Dan."

"What are you trying next?"

"Nothing that would interest you," Wince said. "I found an old adobe shell for sale in Santa Fe. If I can put a small crew together, I'll be up there a while, restoring it. And a new project. Rolan's asked me to build something for an Albuquerque friend of his. I'll keep busy."

"I bet you will." Chutters picked up the empty, pinched it in half, and looked around for a place to put it. He tucked it into his pocket. "New project, huh? Well, good luck with that. But if you decide to come back to Albuquerque, let me know, will you?"

Wince reached out to shake Chutters' hand. "I think you'll know it without me telling you."

"Probably."

"Well...Sorry you made the long drive down here for nothing."

Chutters smiled. "I enjoyed it, in a way. We'll call it my entertainment for the week." He walked to his car.

Chutters sat pondering for a few minutes in the heat. He cracked a window an inch, then started the car, and flipped on the air conditioning. A minute or two would cool his Buick before heading back over the dusty surveyor trail to I-25.

He watched Wince honing the edge on his axe with a whetstone. He thought he might like to try chopping wood sometime. Maybe Wince would lend him an axe. Or buy him one. There was a good chance he could afford it.

Born a Mid-westerner, since 1990 University of New Mexico past-president Richard E. Peck has been a New Mexican. He is a proud grandfather, accomplished speaker and avid story teller, whose *Jackalope Ca$ino* is his 13th book. Other works include five previous novels, 10 produced plays, a score of short stories, collected humor columns, and numerous scholarly essays and reviews.

He and his wife own a hilltop home in Placitas with a 90-mile view in each direction, where he has just completed two new novels, due out in 2011. He plans to keep telling stories and watching the mesa tops toward Cochiti change hue every few minutes of every sunlit New Mexico day.

He can be contacted at www.richardepeck.com.

CPSIA information can be obtained at www.ICGtesting.com
Printed in the USA
LVOW05074522071 2

290937LV00001B/60/P